DESTINATION: GRAND CANYON

by

Thomas E. Way

Dedicated to the memory
of the pathfinders
who blazed the trails to this
grandest canyon of them all.

Golden West Publishers

Cover design by Bruce Robert Fischer/The Art Studio.

Cover photos:

Top: The Grand Canyon (Courtesy Arizona Office of Tourism)

Bottom: Engine #18, shown crossing Cataract Creek on the way to the Grand Canyon. (Photo by Al Richmond. Courtesy Grand Canyon Railway.)

Library of Congress Cataloging-in-Publication Data

Way, Thomas E.
Destination, Grand Canyon: the story of travel to the Grand Canyon / by Thomas E. Way.

p. cm.
Includes bibliographical references.
1. Grand Canyon (Ariz.)—Description and travel. 2. Grand Canyon (Ariz.)—Description and travel—Guide-books. 3. Travelers-Arizona—Grand Canyon—History. I. Title.
F788.W35 1990 90-3100
917.91'32—dc20 CIP
ISBN 0-914846-45-0:

Printed in the United States of America

Golden West Publishers
4113 N. Longview Ave.
Phoenix, AZ 85014, USA
(602) 265-4392

Contents

Foreword

The Majestic Grand Canyon...

This colorful chasm is viewed by boaters on the river—from cars that travel the rim drives—from airplanes and helicopters that provide a bird's-eye-view—or on foot—and for those who desire a more leisurely pace in their sight-seeing schedule, the Canyon may be seen just as many of the oldsters saw it back in Old Cap Hance's day—from the back of a horse or a mule.

Despite all the modern conveyances of travel, the plodding mule still holds his own; many sight-seers enjoy the magnificent view along the trails from the "observation deck" of a mule that holds a higher safety record for passengers than any other available mode of travel.

Getting to the Grand Canyon has not always been easy. It is the intent of this treatise to show some of the trials and tribulations of the past in breaking the trail from afar to get to this grandest of canyons.

Thomas E. Way

I am greatly indebted to Tom, Jr. He wrote the introduction (prehistory) and chapters on the North Rim and Inner Trails.

He also did much research (both legwork and correspondence) on the entire manuscript. He haunted archives and libraries, talked to people far and wide to locate and corroborate dates and pictures to authenticate the story.

T.E.W.

The Beginning: Prehistory

The story of travel to the Grand Canyon is many centuries old. The first to come were prehistoric hunters and gatherers who paused in their wanderings to gaze into the depths and leave their bent-twig animal offerings in caves and under rock overhangs.

Later on, others left pictographs on the rock walls before disappearing into a great silence many centuries long during which the area was empty of all human habitation. In time, the "ancient ones" appeared and they settled, built homes and tended their small garden plots until they, too, passed away, leaving the area strewn with their potsherds and stone walls as monuments to their passing.

In the centuries that followed, other native Americans came and went on errands both spiritual and temporal but apart from the insignificant traces of their trails and campsites on the landscape, the marks of human visitation were hardly noticeable and the Canyon itself remained as it had for eons of time: remote, sublime and mostly unseen by men. . . until the year 1540, when the heralds of a new era appeared in the shape of the first foreign tourists.

During the middle of that year, Francisco Vasquez de Coronado's expedition halted during its exploratory trek near the Hopi pueblos of what is now eastern Arizona and sent out smaller detachments to probe the wilderness. One of the captains of the force, Don Pedro de Tovar,[1] acting on stories heard from the Hopi elders about a vast canyon and a river far away across the plateau to the west, sent a small force under Don Lopez de Cardenas to investigate. Accompanying the force were several Hopi guides who had been impressed for the purpose and these, however unwillingly, conducted their mailed and mounted guests to the very rim of the chasm that no white man's eye had ever seen.

The Spaniards were awestruck. The opposite side of the gorge looked to be "...more than three or four leagues by air line distance away from them" and descent into the gorge, while it looked easy enough from the rim, "proved very hard and difficult."

Some of the more nimble Spaniards tried it and found that while "those who stayed above had estimated that some huge rocks on the sides of the cliffs seemed to be about as tall as a man, ...those who went down swore that when they reached these rocks they were bigger than the great tower of Seville."[2]

Shortly thereafter, the party, by now short of water and defeated in their attempts to reach the river glimmering far below, returned to Hopiland, accompanied by their guides who had neglected to tell of the traditional trails into the Canyon—a place they regarded as sacred.

This first incursion, while it marked the beginning of a new era in the history of what would become the American Southwest, went largely unnoticed there. Succeeding decades and centuries would see the odd exploring party or missionary trek, but by and large, the Spanish, while they "owned" the area, hardly settled north of the Gila River in presentday Arizona and, in fact, seldom visited the northern reaches of the areas that they claimed to rule. The Indians, most of whom had no idea that they were supposed to be subjects of His Most Catholic Majesty, the King of Spain, carried on pretty much as they always had, pausing now and then to visit the Canyon while they went back and forth on their errands as the seasons changed and another two centuries slipped by.

In 1776, while certain events were taking place in Philadelphia, half a continent away, that would have far-reaching effects farther west in another generation, the Canyon received its next European visitor of consequence. This was the Franciscan Father Francisco Garces, who visited the Hualapai and the Havasupai during a missionary journey to the same Hopi pueblos once visited by Coronado. Garces actually climbed down into the western reaches of the Canyon and probably explored the steeper rim areas farther east and he is generally credited with giving the name *Rio Colorado* (Red River) to the silt-laden torrent coursing through the gorge. The padre was apparently well received but since no settlement resulted from his trip and he never returned on a follow-up trek, the impression that he made was fleeting.[3]

In fact, the whole Spanish domination of the Southwest was coming to an end and, in 1821, the entire gigantic piece of real estate came under Mexican rule. The Mexicans were displaced in turn by the Anglo-Americans who were even then pouring westward in a human avalanche. In the vanguard of this migration, and at times even ahead of the vanguard, rode certain bold individuals who would be the next white men to see and marvel at the Grand Canyon.

They were the mountain men, and their travels through the wilderness of western America in search of the fur of the North American beaver took them to many strange and wonderful places, including the great canyon lying far to the west of Santa Fe in New Mexico.

In general, the exact route followed by these men and the adventures that happened along the way can only be conjectured, as most did not leave a written record of their wanderings. The legendary Bill Williams, for instance, may have visited the Canyon, but there is no way of knowing for certain, as he left no sign of his passing which has survived. In this, he was not exceptional, as the usual run of mountain men were rolling stones who gathered no moss and left even fewer monuments to their passing than the Indians who had preceded them. However, there are exceptions to every rule and in the case of mountain men at the Canyon, there is the journal of a young trapper and explorer named James Ohio Pattie.[4]

Pattie, his father, and some other trappers had penetrated into what is now southern Arizona by way of the headwaters of the Gila River as early as 1826. Pushing on into California for more travel and adventure, Pattie eventually headed back east toward Santa Fe by way of the Mohave villages on the Colorado River and the Coconino Plateau. Enroute, he visited the Grand Canyon.

The place's beauty and grandeur moved him not at all. In fact, he saw it as an obstacle to travel and dismissed the whole region

An occasional mountain man paused to gaze across the Grand Canyon. *(Photo by Curtis M. Whitaker)*

as being nearly devoid of anything interesting or valuable enough to prompt a visit! This dismissal was not so much aesthetic as it was practical. Some time later, Pattie and his companions would stumble into the Zuni pueblos of western New Mexico half dead from hunger and thirst, suggesting that their provisions may have been exhausted as they plodded along the waterless rim country, tortured by the sight of the Colorado River glimmering invitingly but unattainably at the bottom of the gorge and that they were just plain too miserable to enjoy the beauties of nature.

On a full stomach and in an "un-dehydrated" condition, Pattie was keen enough to appreciate natural beauty, judging from the number and variety of amorous conquests that he recorded elsewhere in his journal. But, favorably impressed or not, Pattie was probably the first United States' citizen to visit the Grand Canyon who left his name to posterity.

It would be another generation before the next American chronicler and pathfinder turned up and he came part of the way by water. For centuries,[5] explorers had been tracing the route of the Colorado River, trying to determine whether or not the waterway was navigable and if so, to what extent. If waterborne commerce, which at that time was the cheapest and easiest kind available, could ascend the river into the heart of the continent and return bearing the riches of the interior, a very profitable artery of trade could be opened up.

In 1857-58, Lieutenant Joseph Ives of the U.S. Army's Corps of Topographical Engineers, led the first real exploration of the river. Chugging upstream in his steamboat, the *Explorer*, Ives got as far as Black Canyon on the Colorado shores of presentday Mohave County, Arizona, before a submerged rock ended the waterborne portion of the trip. Disembarking and continuing overland on a combined survey and revictualing trip to the Hopi pueblos, Ives reached the Diamond Creek area at the lower west end of the Canyon[6] where he joined the select (and so far, very limited) number of white visitors who had seen the great natural wonder. Ives wasn't too much more favorably impressed than Pattie had been 30-odd years before.

Ives called the region "gloomy and depressing" although to be fair to the young officer, he may have been preoccupied. He had just completed the first leg of a traipse through a semiarid wilderness with a string of thirsty pack animals whose mournful braying had been making the canyons resound and this alone might have put anyone off the scenery!

The Civil War back east halted further exploration of the area for awhile, but with the coming of peace and the resumption of building on the western railroads, interest in the wilderness areas grew apace and prompted a more extensive look at the more remote regions.

In 1869-70, and again in 1871-72, Major John Wesley Powell led boat expeditions down the Colorado from that river's junction with the Green River in southern Wyoming down to its junction with the Virgin River on the Nevada border. Powell and his men surveyed, mapped, photographed, sketched and collected specimens all along the route and these items would later prove most valuable. From the standpoint of navigability and potential as a trade artery, the Colorado was a disappointment. The stretches of rapids and white water along its upper course made it unusable for steamboats even though steamboat traffic linked settlements all along its lower course and would continue to do so even long after the coming of the railroads.[7]

Powell's findings were summarized in ***Canyons of the Colorado*** and other works and these reports, plus the photographs and sketches and the samples of flora and fauna stimulated much interest; some of it aesthetic, but more of it practical. The Canyon looked as if it might contain mineral wealth and where there was money to be made by rock scratching, the scratchers would be sure to follow!

Beginning about 1880, various prospectors set to work in and around the Canyon, staking claims on what was then open public land. These men required both a means of supplying their necessities and a way of shipping the fruits of their labor to the outside world. These needs were met by wagoners and packers operating from the railhead towns along the course of the advancing Atlantic and Pacific Railroad some 70 miles to the south. At first, the traffic was all supplies one way and smelter-bound ore the other way, but in time, various people began making the trip. Mostly, these were other prospectors or potential investors. Occasionally there would be a representative from the newly-evolved species of "tourist."

Up until then, "tourism," as that term is now understood, hardly existed in the American West. Most people did not have the necessary leisure, funds or inclination to indulge in travel for its own sake. The means of getting about were still slow, uncomfortable and primitive and the Indian populations still too restive to encourage gadding around just to look at scenery if one didn't happen to be interested in doing anything to or with that landscape. Undeveloped land was considered useless in its pristine state, and even the artists and naturalists who had been out prowling around the frontiers since the days of Catlin and Bodmer, had been doing so as often as not to publicize the raw land in the hope that their pictures and reports would stimulate immigration by settlers who would do something "worthwhile" with the land.

With the creation of the first national park at Yellowstone in 1872 and perhaps the dawning realization that the riches of creation were not infinite after all and ought to be preserved to some extent "just to be looked at and enjoyed," a new class of traveler came West. Coincidentally, this newly-minted desire to see and enjoy natural wonders dovetailed neatly with the closing of the frontier, the shrinkage of Indian conflicts in size and frequency, and the post-Civil War expansion of the railroads to the hitherto remoter regions. With the desire to go made possible of realization by the existence of the means, many of the better-heeled gentry back east headed for the territories to gaze upon what they'd only read about for years.

Meanwhile, back at the Grand Canyon, it hadn't taken many of the prospectors long to figure out that there had to be an easier way to make a living than battering away with a pick and shovel for the ever-elusive mineral riches.

No one knows now which one of the rock scratching pioneers at the great gorge was first to gaze upon a tourist, realize that the tourist had to be fed and sheltered and guided to and fro while he or she was actually at the Canyon, not to mention being transported back and forth from the train to the rim, and realize, too, that a respectable amount of money could be made from the activity.

Once the realization sank in though, a number of men put their prospecting on the back burner and went to "wrangling dudes." It was this group of hardy entrepreneurs who launched the next phase of the story of travel to the Grand Canyon.

Thomas E. Way, Jr.

NOTES

1. Pedro de Tovar later achieved immortality in the annals of the Grand Canyon tourist trade by having the El Tovar Hotel named in his honor.

2. Passages describing the activities of the Cardenas detachment which are enclosed in quotation marks are summarized from the April 1984, ***Arizona Highways*** article "In Coronado's Footsteps" and are taken from the writings of Coronado's two soldier chroniclers, Pedro de Casteneda, and Juan Jaramillo. While the exact length of a league varied somewhat from country to country during the Age of Discovery and the Spanish colonial period in the Americas, the average was about three miles to a league.

3. Francisco Garces was killed by the Yuma Indians in 1781 just north of presentday Yuma, Arizona. This event, for all intents and purposes, marked the end of the colonial mission period in Arizona.

4. Pattie's journal was first published in 1831 by Timothy Flint of Cincinnati and entitled ***The Personal Narrative of James O. Pattie***. The book has since gone through five revival printings, the most recent one in 1962.

5. In conjunction with Coronado's expedition, Hernando de Alarcon sailed two small ships loaded with provisions for Coronado's force from Acapulco, up the Sea of Cortez, to the mouth of the Colorado in the summer of 1540. Pushing on in small boats, Alarcon and his men got as far as the confluence with the Gila. Failing to contact Coronado, Alarcon and his men returned home, having been the first Europeans to set foot in the future province of Upper California.

6. Diamond Creek's junction with the Colorado is the present western terminus of many of the river running trips and was at one time, the site of the Farlee Hotel, first tourist accommodation in the Grand Canyon.

7. Steamboat traffic regularly plied the Colorado between Port Isabel, at the river's mouth on the Sea of Cortez, and the presentday ghost town site of Hardyville, Arizona—a distance of nearly 500 miles. Some boats got as far as Callville, a Mormon settlement now submerged by Lake Mead, but a regular schedule of sailings to the latter seems never to have been current. The coming of the railroads slowly eroded the steamboat's business and by the second decade of the 20th century, they were gone for good.

The Prospectors

The Grand Canyon has long been a place of mystery. In 1540 one Garcia Lopez de Cardenas and his small band of weary conquistadors searched vainly for a way to reach the other side of this colorful chasm, "at least four leagues across," or the river in the bottom, shimmering in the sun, tantalizingly out of reach. This same Grand Canyon has hypnotized and mystified those who have since gazed into its depths.

Nearly four centuries later, the only people who saw the Canyon were the aboriginal Indians who lived in the area or nomadic bands migrating to and from their hunting grounds.

In the mid-1860's our government took a renewed interest in the western states. Geological and cartographical surveying expeditions were sent west to study the earth's structure and map it for the statistical records. In 1869, John Wesley Powell led an expedition on a marine approach to and through the Grand Canyon by river. He undoubtedly found the Colorado River to be a rough and uncompromisingly dangerous vantage point from which to view this spectacular canyon.

The average sight-seer nowadays seeks a different, less adventurous approach to the canyon rather than by boat on the turbulent river. Some thrill-seekers, however, still book passage with river runners who have the necessary equipment for the occasion. The old boats have been replaced by large inflatable rubber rafts that furnish a higher degree of safety for those who choose to "rough-it" down the Colorado River. The construction of Glen Canyon Dam has shortened the river trip somewhat.

As time passed, an occasional prospector, cowboy or sheepman paused in his wanderings to view the incomparable spectacle. The Kolb Brothers, Ellsworth and Emery, went into the photographic business at Grand Canyon in 1902. They had bought the equipment of a Williams photographer who was going out of business in Williams, Arizona.

Emery Kolb had been a photographer in Pennsylvania before he and his brother came west. They set up a business on the rim of the Canyon where they took pictures of the few adventurers who rode mules down the Bright Angel Trail.

In 1911 they had special boats built with which to make a picture-taking river voyage through Grand Canyon. They not only conquered the rampaging river but took moving pictures of the trip and surrounding scenery as they progressed along the route.

The Kolb brothers made other boat trips through the Canyon in 1921 and 1923 and again in 1928—the latter trip was in search of a couple, Glen and Bessie Hyde, who were celebrating their

Emery Kolb (at left) and Ellsworth Kolb (holding the oar) photographed during the search for the Hyde party.
(Santa Fe Railroad Collection, NAU Special Collections Library, Northern Arizona University, Flagstaff)

honeymoon with a boat trip down the Colorado River. Their boat was located but neither of the couple was ever found.

The Kolbs built a studio on the edge of the Canyon, overlooking the head of Bright Angel Trail—"Cameron Trail" at that time. While the studio was under construction, the Kolbs rented one of the tents at nearby Bright Angel Tent City, from which to operate their business. On the completion of the studio and for many years thereafter the mules of the guided trail rides stopped with their passengers at a measured distance from the studio and, from an open window, Kolb took a picture of the party. Emery Kolb then took the negatives down the trail afoot to Indian Gardens (4½ miles distant) where he developed the film. Then he took the film back up the trail to the studio where pictures were printed for the trail riders on their return.

It was said that Emery had a pace somewhere between a walk and a trot that covered the trail faster than the mules. As more mule trains used the trail, Emery made the trip twice a day.

After the Santa Fe started hauling water from Del Rio Springs, one hundred and twenty miles away, to service Grand Canyon's needs, Emery still, for many years, ran his film down to Indian Gardens where they had built a small shack near the springs.

In 1974, at age 93, Emery Kolb made a final nostalgic trip down the river; that time he was in one of the modern inflatable rafts—"not like the old days—" he later remarked.

So much to be seen by so few through the years created the desire of those few to bring the Canyon within the reach of many. The ultimate goal could be reached only by the offer of a more trouble-free form of access to this greatest of the world's natural wonders. So far the horse, or horse-drawn equipment, had furnished the only method of transportation.

The role of the horse has changed significantly through the years; literally, he has changed ends. Once he was in harness at the front of the moving vehicle. Now he rides in regal splendor in a trailer behind the vehicle. Apparently all concerned, including the horse, are happy with this inevitable progression in the annals of locomotion.

Before the rails came, transcontinental travel was by stage-

Cameron Hotel and original Kolb Studio, circa 1903.
(Photo courtesy Northern Arizona Pioneers Historical Society. NAU Special Collections Library, Flagstaff)

coach or wagon train. Even if the weary travelers had known of the existence of this canyon few, if any, would have strayed from the established cross-country route to see it. Transportation and travel were just not that enjoyable. Why add those extra miles of unnecessary hardship onto an already tortuous schedule?

Favorable reports emanating from Powell's exploration down the Colorado River stimulated the interest of prospectors, who invaded the reachable side canyons and ramparts of the Canyon in search of riches. For several years thereafter the beauty of the Canyon was of secondary interest. The mineral wealth and getting it out of the Canyon was all important.

Ralph Camerom came to the Canyon in 1883 where his brother, Niles, later joined him. Their primary interest was mining. In order to get the ore out of the Canyon, they renovated and developed the old trail that had been originally used by the Havasupai Indians many years ago. He was aided in this trail construction by Pete Berry, a fellow prospector. From time to time other prospectors aided in the renovation of the trail that was dubbed "Cameron Trail" and for several years Cameron charged a toll for its use.

This trail was later acquired by Coconino County, which was carved from part of Yavapai County in 1891. By the mid 1890's the trail was gaining recognition as a tourist attraction by which one might "better explore the inner beauty of the Canyon."

In 1889 Robert Brewster Stanton led a party of surveyors from Green River, Utah, down the river through the Grand Canyon, to Diamond Creek. Stanton had been in Powell's second expedition down the Colorado River through Grand Canyon. This voyage was under the sponsorship of one Frank Brown, president of a Denver-based railway company. The purpose of the survey was to locate a river-level railway through the Grand Canyon. Coal from western Colorado mines could be shipped to California by way of this shorter route.

News of that proposed railway encouraged geologists and prospectors to explore the possibilities of mineral wealth in the Canyon. With a shorter convenient railway system, mining would be profitable. This would enable prospectors to bring out their ore and develop the mines. The traces of silver, gold and copper did not warrant working the claims without the transportation of ore by a nearby railroad.

From the start, the Stanton expedition was doomed to failure. Brown, president of the railway, went along on the trip. He was killed in an accident soon after the trip started. Two other members of the crew were drowned before the ill-fated voyage was over. The main thing the expedition discovered was that there would never be a railroad built through the Grand Canyon.

After the Stanton expedition failed to find a suitable location for a railroad in the Canyon, Ralph Cameron lost interest in mining. The number of prospectors who were searching for riches in the Canyon diminished. Only a few of the hard-rock breed remained when the possibility of a nearby railroad failed to bear fruit. Most of the prospecting population looked elsewhere for a livelihood. Some found that catering to the tourist trade was a far more profitable pursuit than prospecting

Mrs. Farrell and Mrs. Straight in front of the Cameron Hotel and post office about 1903. *(Courtesy National Park Service, Grand Canyon National Park)*

for minerals.

In general, very little high-grade copper ore came out of the Canyon although one particular ore sample from the Last Chance claim, under Grand View Point, was adjudged the highest grade copper ore submitted for inspection at the 1898 World's Fair in Chicago. The trouble, was, that unless the ore could be efficiently moved to a smelter, it lost much of its potential value.

Cameron moved up onto the rim and built a hotel west of Buckey O'Neill's cabin, near the head of the Cameron Trail, where he could keep an eye on traffic and collect tolls.

Cameron's fighting with the railroad and Fred Harvey over

property use along the rim went on for years. Eventually, Cameron sold his hotel to Harvey and part of the building was incorporated into the fabric of the Bright Angel Lodge. After Cameron's departure from the Canyon, the Cameron Trail was renamed the Bright Angel Trail.

The name "Bright Angel" is said to have originated during one of John Wesley Powell's expeditions. The sylvan appearance of the mouth of what is now Bright Angel Creek in the inner gorge, with its lush green trees and undergrowth amid the parched surroundings is said to have suggested the name. To offset the stigma of a creek farther up the river that bore the name "Dirty Devil Creek," this new watercourse was christened "Bright Angel Creek."

The name was eventually attached to the trail and hotel and the North Rim has a "Bright Angel Point," near the head of the creek by the same name. It appears that the angels now have the situation pretty well in hand!

The beginning of the 1890's saw a growing number of prospectors seeking a change of occupation. William Bass founded a resort camp and a stagecoach connection to and from Williams (and later Ashfork) to bring in guests and sightseers. In addition, Bass constructed over 50 miles worth of trails in the Canyon itself, including the stretch that survives as the present-day Bass Trail. At the river crossing of this trail, Bass built a cable tramway capable of holding one mule or several people at once. On the other side, his trail continued to the North Rim.

Another prospector-turned-dude wrangler was Louis D. Boucher. Arriving at the Canyon about 1891, he entered the tourist business almost immediately, diversifying his pursuits to include orchard-tending and vegetable gardening in addition to prospecting and tourist tending. Boucher built the last of the privately-constructed inner-canyon trails from the rim down to Dripping Springs and his own near-the-river tourist stop along the watercourse later named Boucher Creek.

Dan Hogan gave up his Canyon claim in 1898 and answered the call for volunteers when the Spanish-American War broke out. Going to Prescott, he enlisted in the First U.S. Volunteer Cavalry which was then familiarly referred to as "Teddy's

Terrors" (after the unit's second-in-command, Teddy Roosevelt). Later on, the group became known as the "Rough Riders" and it was in Cuba that Hogan became friends with Roosevelt, the soon-to-be President of the United States. When the war was over, Hogan drifted back to the Canyon where he staked another claim—this one on the West Rim. This mine still produces ore.

John "Cap" Hance had claims in the Canyon below the East Rim and William H. "Bill" Ashurst worked his claims down near the Colorado River.

Ashurst, father of the late Senator Henry Fountain Ashurst, actively worked his claims but never found ore rich enough to warrant hauling out by pack-burro, the only method of transportation feasible at that time. He was later struck and killed by a landslide near his mine in an accident that was surrounded by an aura of mystery—never completely clarified.

Aside from an occasional small "rich pocket" none of the "in-canyon" claims showed high grade ore. Very few copper-

Coconino Cycle Club at Grand Canyon in 1897. *(From G. K. Woods collection, photographer unknown)*

ore-laden burro packtrains ever emerged from Grand Canyon. Most of these burros were either freed or escaped and eventually formed the nucleus of today's feral burro population in Grand Canyon.

Even as the prospectors gave up on finding riches, the beauty of the Canyon was starting to bring travelers from near and far—some on bicycles—

Although many cyclists have through the years pedalled their way, singly and in groups, to Grand Canyon, probably the first organized group to have that distinction was the Coconino Cycling Club in Flagstaff. This club was organized in 1893. For several years they made an "Annual Run" to Grand Canyon. Instructions issued before the fourth Annual Run for the benefit of those who intended to make the trip in 1897 were:

> DATE—The start will be made at 6 o'clock a.m. from the rooms of the Coconino Cycling Club Flagstaff, Arizona, September 7th. The 8th, 9th and 10th will be spent at the Canyon, and the return trip made on the 11th.
>
> DISTANCE—The distance to the hotel at the Canyon is about seventy miles. The trip can be made in from eight to twelve hours, according to the speed and endurance of the rider. Any good amateur rider can make the ride in from ten to twelve hours.
>
> ROAD—The road is good and level, in the main, although there are some heavy grades on it. It winds among the foothills and over the lower slopes of the San Francisco Mountains for the first twenty to twenty-five miles, passing through a fine forest of pine for this distance. The succeeding twenty-five miles leads through a rolling prairie region, and for the remainder of the distance the road runs through the Coconino Forest, which here skirts the rim of the Canyon for several miles.
>
> EXPENSE—The Coconino Cycling Club will arrange and meet all expenses of the run, charging each participant $11.00. This will include sleeping accommodations and board at the Canyon, meals en route and transportation for baggage not to exceed twenty-five pounds, but does not include expenses at Flagstaff.
>
> MISCELLANEOUS—In order to insure accommodations, notice should be sent to the secretary of the Club by September 1st of intention to participate in the run. The Club will endeavor to arrange for all who may come, but will not guarantee accommodations for any who may send their names later than the date above mentioned.
>
> Riders will find it much to their advantage to fit wheels used on this trip with gear not exceeding 66, and also with coasters and brake.

Dr. P. A. Melick with his motorcycle on the rim in 1905. Original photo by Kolb. *(From the collection of Dr. D. W. Melick, Phoenix)*

In 1905 Dr. P. A. Melick, pioneer Williams physician, rode, shoved and coaxed his Pierce motorcycle over the trail from Williams to the Grand Canyon. It started as a pleasure jaunt but due to a malfunctioning cycle plus the rugged terrain of hills and other hazards of the trail, the journey turned into a nightmare. He thought seriously several times along the trail of shoving the cantankerous bike off a cliff and completing the journey afoot.

In spite of the lack of power in the "one-lunger" engine and the other hazards of the trail, Dr. Melick completed the trip. That was the first motorcycle on the rim of the Grand Canyon.

Emery Kolb, pioneer photographer at the Canyon, took Dr. Melick's picture with his cycle, on the Canyon's rim near the newly-constructed El Tovar Hotel. The El Tovar had just been completed and opened to the public in 1905.

John G. Verkamp was an earlyday inhabitant of Grand Canyon. Before the turn of the century, he established the first curio business at the Canyon in one of the tents of Tent City, where the present Bright Angel Lodge now stands. There was not enough business to support the enterprise at that time so he sold his stock to Martin Buggeln, the manager of Tent City, and moved back to Flagstaff.

Another mining "land rush" came along in 1905, when the El Tovar was completed. Mining claims were being filed along the rim and Verkamp came back to the Canyon to take part in the scramble for choice rim land by filing a claim east of the newly-constructed El Tovar and the then-building Hopi House. By then, Santa Fe trains were bringing more people to the Canyon and the curio business boomed. Verkamp constructed a permanent store building in 1906 and the Verkamp family is still in business there today, a couple of generations later.

Most of the "on-the-rim" mining claims were later taken over by the Santa Fe/Fred Harvey empire but Verkamp hung on by maintaining residence on his land. Actually, the only mining claim on the rim that really showed workable mineral traces was Dan Hogan's claim, west of the Village. None of the other rim claims showed enough traces of "pay dirt" to substantiate the mining claims of their owners.

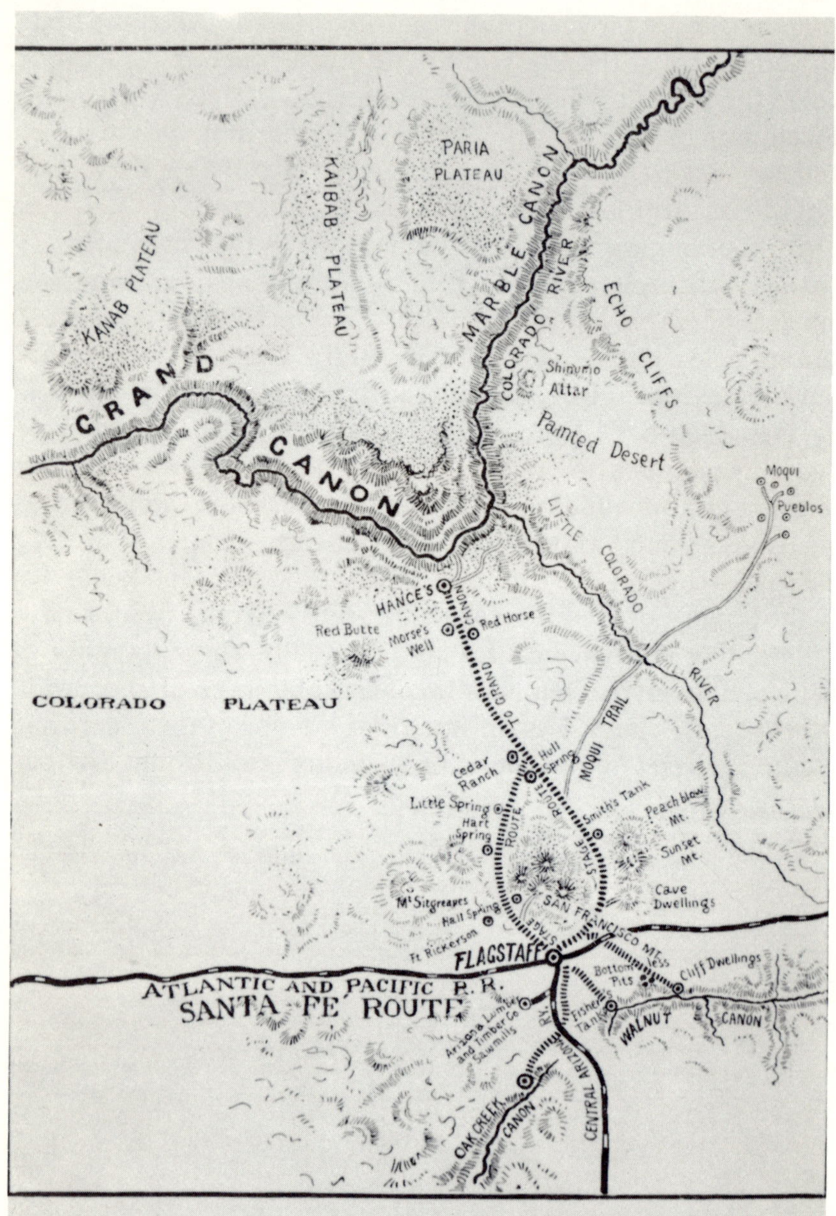

Map of Flagstaff-Grand Canyon stage routes, 1893. *(From C. A. Higgins' book Grand Canyon of the Colorado River, Arizona, published by AT & SF RR, Chicago)*

Stagecoaches

There was still a shortage of visitors to Grand Canyon until the mid-1880s. The era of stagecoach travel to the Canyon started after 1883 when the Atlantic & Pacific laid its rails across Northern Arizona. The first stages operated from four stations—Peach Springs, Ashfork, Williams and Flagstaff.

J. H. Farlee had a stage line from Peach Springs to the lower end of Grand Canyon, where he built a small hotel near the confluence of Diamond Creek and the Colorado River. Farlee's Hotel was described by a traveler as a "little one-room board shanty with a lean-to on the back that served as a cook shack."

Diamond Creek also served as a check point for some river boats and "end-of-journey" for others, though not many river runners braved the perils of the Colorado River at that time. It was also a place where horse-thieves were known at times of low water to drive stolen herds of horses across the river; this was the only crossing considered semi-safe within many miles.

The Diamond Creek (Farlee's) Hotel was only 23 miles from Peach Springs. The less scenic area soon lost its popularity and tourists sought the more spectacular portion of the Canyon—although it meant a much longer journey in a stagecoach from the other stage stations, located east of Peach Springs.

In 1885 John "Cap" Hance and William Hull began catering to the tourist trade. They established a passenger service between Flagstaff and the Grand Canyon[1]. These early-day entrepreneurs inaugurated and put into service two made-over farm wagons. The charge for the round trip was $20, without meals. One had to take along his own meals. The schedule was irregular—when enough passengers were found to "make a load," the stage left on the trip.

In May 1892, the Grand Canyon Stage Line opened for business, incorporating Hance and Hull's enterprise. The new company, which was actually controlled by the Atlantic & Pacific Railroad, then worked out a schedule and built and

Farlee Hotel near Diamond Creek and the Colorado River. Picture taken about 1920. *(Courtesy Mohave County Historical Society)*

staffed relay stations.

Hance at this time was still operating his hotel/tourist camp east of Grandview and guiding parties of sightseers into the Canyon via the Hance Trail. He was still a guide and pathfinder too as is evidenced by the ads he ran from time to time in the ***Flagstaff Champion***:

> "...Being thoroughly conversant with all the trails leading to the Grand Canyon of the Colorado, I am prepared to conduct parties thereto at any time. I have a fine spring of water near my house on the rim of the Canyon, and can furnish accommodations for tourists and their animals."

The Grand Canyon Stage Line became a well-organized transportation system and had a regular schedule worked out by the end of 1892. In the beginning, there were three relay stops for passengers resting and horse changing: Little Springs, 16 miles northwest of Flagstaff; Cedar Station, 18 miles beyond that; and Moqui Station, 20 miles north of Cedar. Cedar Station was the lunch stop (50¢ per meal) and Hance's hotel and tent complex at the rim was the Grand Canyon terminus where the evening meal and a night's lodging were available for $1.

The advertised trail schedule was: "Four and six-horse

coaches leave Flagstaff Mondays, Wednesdays and Fridays, 7 a.m. Thirty minute stop at Cedar Springs for dinner. Return Tuesdays, Thursdays and Saturdays. Excellent hotel accommodations at Canyon in connection with Stage Line."

The trail from Flagstaff to Grandview Point covered about 75 miles of rough, rocky terrain and the drivers had their hands full dodging rocks and trees as there was no real road, at least recognizable as such, over much of the route.

For the most part the stagecoaches were cumbersome. Where there was no existing road, the horses and heavy conveyances broke their own trail by heading in the general direction of their destination and plowing forward. After a few trips, the ruts were so noticeable as to make it impossible for anyone behind to lose the way.

The journey took from 10 to 14 hours if all went well. . . much longer if there was trouble (a wheel might fall off or break, etc.). In case of accidents, passengers were expected to help the driver by dismounting and rendering all possible assistance. Even when the going was accident-free, there was little comfort in the ride. One oldtimer, thinking back on some of his bygone experiences, reminisced almost wistfully, ". . . an Indian attack or a holdup would have been a welcome diversion on most of them bone-bustin' trips!"

William Wallace "Billy" Bass came to Williams in 1883 and started a livery service.[2] In 1885, he launched a stagecoach service from Williams to Grand Canyon using a new trail which ran northwest from Williams, by way of Cataract Canyon, to a camp on the west rim of the Canyon.[3] This camp, named Bass Camp, was augmented several years later, in the mid-1890s, by the small wooden Bass Hotel. Before this though, Bass had begun a regularly scheduled stagecoach service from Williams to the Grand Canyon in late 1891 which replaced the earlier "according to need and appearance of passengers" service of 1885. In 1892, Bass sold his Williams Livery to Sanford Rowe but retained management of the stage line.

In 1892, Fernando R. "Ferd" Nellis started a stage line from Williams to Grand Canyon. This line used a different route via Rhoades (later named Maine and still later, Parks) to the

Billy Bass puts diamond hitch on pack burro for a trip into the Grand Canyon. *(From the W. W. Bass Collection)*

vicinity of Grandview, and operated on a tri-weekly schedule.[4] The Williams to Grand Canyon run over this route took a minimum of 10 hours (with luck). The last 20 miles of this route and the last leg of the trail from Flagstaff merged and ended near Grandview.

Before hotel accommodations were available, a second wagon was usually hauled along behind the coach as a trailer. Under this contingency, two or more horses were added to the hitch. The trailer was laden with bedrolls for the passengers and driver, provisions, dutch ovens and other cooking paraphernalia, and hay and grain for the team. Water barrels took up the rest of the space. In case of a serious breakdown or accident along the way, the driver and passengers would be able to manage while awaiting assistance that was often several days in coming.

In the embryonic period of these stage lines, horses were changed three times (occasionally four) during the trip.

Originally, on both of the Williams-Grand Canyon routes (the Flagstaff line was the same), large corrals were maintained at the relay stations. The incoming teams would be fed and watered and turned loose in the usually pasture-sized corrals until another coach needed them. The incoming team would then be replaced by a fresh team to continue the journey. Buildings were erected later at most relay points and staffed with the necessary personnel to care for the stock and maintain the schedules.

The driver of the incoming stage was always careful to keep one of his present team horses to ride in rounding up a fresh change of teams. Most drivers, being cowboys, possessed the universal aversion for walking shared by all cowboys; the high heels worn by a cowboy were not conducive to hiking in a rocky pasture. Some of these pastures were quite large and the horses liked their freedom—many were still half-wild.

On occasion, a gate might have been unintentionally left open or a fence broken down. This, of course, occasioned a delay in the schedule while the driver and volunteers among the passengers mounted the already-weary stage horses and went in search of the missing horses; sometimes this was no small undertaking.

Early-day stagecoaches to Grand Canyon did not maintain the "hell-for-leather" schedule depicted in song and legend. Indians were peaceable in the area. The only other menace from man would be a holdup and that seldom happened—as far as can be ascertained, that never occurred on the Grand Canyon haul. Road conditions over most of the route did not permit a fast pace.

On one occasion (probably one of many) a stage driver shot from atop the stage and killed a deer. While the passengers waited and watched, the driver cleaned out the deer and loaded it in with the luggage belonging to the passengers.

"I need some meat at home," was his explanation to his amazed captive audience. Often those riding "on top" practiced their marksmanship by shooting jackrabbits from the moving vehicle. The stagecoaches did however maintain an amazingly accurate schedule, all things considered—rain storms, break-

Capt. John Hance
(G. K. Woods collection, photographer unknown)

downs, etc., were an anticipated hazard and taken in stride.

There was a continued rivalry between the various stage lines. Both Williams Stage lines added new coaches on their services. The Flagstaff-based Grand Canyon Stage Line advertised a lower fare; "a round-trip to Grand Canyon for $15." They also advertised—"horses, vehicles, competent drivers and guides furnished at reasonable rates. Special attention given to tourists wishing to visit any point of interest."

Cap Hance added improvements to his hotel and added several tents to his tent city at Grandview; no longer would these tourists have to brave the elements if a sudden storm arose—Hance so advised his clientele.

Hance's dubious fame arose from his penchant for telling tall tales. He was Grand Canyon's answer to the fabled Baron Munchausen of a century before—only the setting was changed. Some years later Hance was employed by Fred Harvey to regale visitors with his famous, but seldom true, stories of Grand Canyon. Who could better fulfill this mission than he who had professed to having dug this famous landmark and with the resulting debris had fashioned the mountains of the surrounding country?

Among old-timers in Northern Arizona, the name Cap Hance is still synonymous with the fabrication of some impossibly bizarre, unbelievable tale. That facet of his life is remembered with far more clarity than is his serious side—his important role in the early-day development of tourist facilities at Grand Canyon.

Somewhere along the line this self-administered notoriety must have had far-reaching results. On May 10, 1897, he succeeded in getting a postoffice established at that location (Grandview) and himself duly appointed postmaster.[5] This appointment was probably due largely to his having the only building available at that location for that enterprise. Thus "Tourist" became the first postoffice at Grand Canyon. It has been contended by some that this postoffice was not officially sanctioned by proper circles in Washington, D.C., but merely a local arrangement doing business between Flagstaff and Grandview Point.

Hance's hotel and tourist camp at Grand Canyon, circa 1890-1900. *(G. K. Woods Collection)*

Arizona Territory: Post Offices and Postmasters, by John and Lillian Theobald, lists Tourist as an officially-designated postoffice, further stating—"as the name (Tourist) implies, this was the goal of tourists brought to the brink of the Grand Canyon by John Hance, the pioneer guide and famed raconteur who first exploited this natural wonder as a tourist attraction." This postoffice was discontinued April 12, 1899.[6]

In 1892, Nellis sold out his stage line to Sanford Rowe, who had previously acquired Bass' livery stable in Williams. Early in the life of this stage line Rowe homesteaded an area three miles west of the present Grand Canyon Village; this was later and still is known as Rowe's Well. Eventually Rowe sold out the Williams Livery and Stage Line to Martin Buggeln, a pioneer railroader, deputy sheriff and cattleman.

In 1894, Billy Bass moved the southern terminus of his stage line from Williams to Ash Fork.[7] Although the trail was somewhat longer, he claimed it was a better all-weather approach to the Canyon. This trail joined his former Williams-Grand Canyon road about thirty miles north of Ash Fork. This new route had an additional significant value; his stages met the trains of the Santa Fe, Prescott & Phoenix Line, locally called the "Pea-Vine," where it joined the Atlantic & Pacific mainline in Ash Fork, thus drawing on tourist trade of central and southern Arizona.

Bass inserted an ad in the ***Weekly Arizona Miner*** (Prescott) April 15, 1895:

> Cataract route, formerly the Williams route. On May 1st and until further notice I will run regular stages between Ash Fork and the Grand Canyon of the Colorado River. Tourists are landed directly opposite Point Sublime at the head of Mystic Spring Trail reaching the Cliff Dwellings, Grand scenic divide, Rains of Paradise, and Colorado River on horseback. No rope ladders or toboggan slides by this route. Cataract Canyon, Supai Villages and Bridal Veil Falls reached by this route only. A commodious hotel, under the Harvey Eating House management, is now open in Ash Fork for the accommodation of this class of travel. Rates—$3.00 per day. The Santa Fe, Prescott & Phoenix makes liberal concessions to parties of 10 or more. For rates apply to F. A. Healy, G. P.A. (general passenger agent), Prescott, or any agent of that line. I will run stages to suit the convenience of my patrons. Stage fare, round trip $15. Parties of 10 or more, $12.50. Meals and beds, 75¢ each. For further information please address
>
> W. W. Bass, prop. Ash Fork, A. T.

Billy Bass, driver, with a load of tourists near Bass Camp, about 1890. *(From the W. W. Bass Collection)*

From the mid-1890s until the coming of the rails to Grand Canyon a few years later there were three stage companies vying for the tourist trade between the three railheads and Grand Canyon. The Flagstaff stage line continued to prosper. Buggeln continued operating his "shorter—direct route" from Williams and Bass operated out of Ash Fork with his "all-weather" route. Peach Springs had given up operating the stage line from that point to the Colorado River.

Buggeln added new, modern coaches to the line to better contend with the competition. As a further inducement to coax the traveler into adding the Grand Canyon to his itinerary, he built a two-story hotel near the Hance hotel at Grandview. This new structure was the ultra-modern hostelry of the day. It was thought at the time that this would be the center of activity in the future development of south rim tourist accommodations.

These hotels (Buggeln's and Hance's) served Grand Canyon travelers for several years before it was known that the railroad of the future would approach the present location (present-day Grand Canyon Village).

Buggeln Hotel at Grand Canyon. Photo was taken just before demolition by National Park Service. *(Photographer: David Eiting)*

The few passengers who braved the rigors of the bouncing stagecoaches were but a drop in the bucket. It was, however, the only mode of public transportation available to the Canyon for anyone who lived away from the area. Comparatively few persons risked life and limb to see the Canyon.

William Randolph Hearst, a young New York newspaper publisher just starting out in the business, visited Grand Canyon.[8] His glowing accounts of the scenery published in the ***New York Journal***, (he smoothed over the hardships of the stagecoach ride) were read far and wide.

William Owen "Buckey" O'Neill, newspaper publisher, lawman, miner, mayor, soldier of fortune and sometimes opportunist, read Hearst's inspiring account with interest. Leaving his Prescott interest temporarily behind, he visited the Canyon.

He liked it so well he built a log cabin on the rim where Bright Angel Lodge now stands and a bunkhouse farther back in the cedars. This particular location was chosen for the cabin due to its proximity to the head of Bright Angel Trail (at that time "Cameron Trail"). These original buildings are still units of the Bright Angel Lodge complex.

Buckey O'Neill cabin is now divided into two units, both affording one of the most spectacular views of the Grand Canyon available. As you leave the lobby of the present lodge (Bright Angel), on the side facing the Canyon, Buckey's cabin is immediately on your left, about twenty yards distant.

O'Neill looked beyond the beauty of the scenery. Entrepreneur that he was, his past experience in mining stood him in good stead. Outcroppings of copper ore were visible almost everywhere. In his initial excitement he also braved the depths of the Canyon and eventually filed on a promising claim at the base of the colorful minaret that later became known as O'Neill Butte.

The richest deposits of copper were above the canyon's rim. The surrounding area seemed to be an almost endless series of rich copper pockets in a mostly limestone formation or base.

Ralph Cameron took an active interest in promoting a larger hotel to complement O'Neill's meager quarters. The hue and cry

Old Bright Angel Lodge with O'Neill cabin at right. Photo taken before 1898. *(Courtesy National Park Service, Grand Canyon National Park)*

was taken up by interested parties. The ***Williams News*** of May 8, 1897, stated, under the heading: "Grand View Hotel (not to be confused with Grandview, 14 miles east)—"Projected Building At The Grand Canyon's Brink—"

> The matter of a tourists hotel at the Grand Canyon assumed definite shape this week when the ground at the brink of the great wonder, near the Bright Angel Trail, was surveyed and located as a mineral claim. This was done by the citizens of Williams to forestall the designs of other parties, who threatened to begin operations.
>
> The plan contemplates a commodious building of dressed lumber, including all necessary appointments and accessories. The center of the hotel will be a court 28x20 feet overlooking the Canyon at one of the most desirable scenic points. The location is near Rowe's Well. It is known variously as Observation Point, Five Points, and Rowe's Point.
>
> When tourists know that they can secure proper accommodations and comfort during inclement weather, more of them will go to the Canyon than before. Those who have been to the Canyon can readily imagine the pleasure of looking out upon its bewildering glories from the hotel windows. The citizens have taken hold of the proposition with the proper spirit and no doubt the subscription paper that will be circulated will be liberally signed. Sanford Rowe will transport the lumber, and the expense from that source will not figure in the total.

Upon completion of this hotel, Cameron gave up the tourist promotion business and went into politics. From Grand Canyon he went back to Flagstaff. In 1896 he successfully sought the office of Sheriff of Coconino County and his term of office started on January 1, 1897. In the early 1900s he ran for and was elected county supervisor. From then on he held various territorial offices and finally, after statehood (1912) he served as United States Senator between 1920 and 1927.

Ralph Cameron, Sheriff of Coconino County *(Courtesy Northern Arizona Pioneers' Historical Society—Northern Arizona University Library)*

As the stagecoach industry improved through the years, the stage trails were also worked on only enough to permit continued travel. After a particularly violent rainstorm there were washouts; large boulders had to be removed or recovered with dirt. Most of this labor was done by the drivers, while the stage load of passengers looked on. On occasion the tourists pitched in and helped. There was no regular road crew.

In the later days of stagecoach travel, the coaches were more comfortable to ride in. The roads had been smoothed out somewhat and the automobile was in the near offing as a means of travel. Despite some advances though, a stage ride was still a long way from being a "limousine and bon-bon" vacation. The Grand Canyon Stage Line had some six-horse stages that were twice the length of the four-horse vehicles. The longer wheel base furnished a more comfortable ride and the bigger size could accommodate more passengers.

G. K. Woods was general manager of the Grand Canyon Stage Line and in 1899 he had a book published entitled ***Personal Impressions of the Grand Canyon of the Colorado . . .*** This volume was a combined promotional ad for the stage line

G. K. Woods, manager of the Grand Canyon Stage Line.
(Photo from the G. K. Woods Collection)

J. Wilbur Thurber, proprietor, Flagstaff-Grand Canyon stage line.
(From the G. K. Woods collection)

and compendium of several years worth of signatures and comments of people who had stayed at John Hance's hotel/tent village east of Grandview.

Woods was skeptical and probably a little alarmed by advance notices of the capabilities of the newfangled automobiles which were being touted by their makers and sellers as the next glorious step in the evolution of travel. One subtle advertisement for the stage line in his book read: ". . . The trip can be made by the latest mode of transportation—the Auto-Mobile Carriage—or by the well-tried and thoroughly reliable Concord coach, which is the chief equipment of J. Wilbur Thurber's Grand Canyon Stage Line."

The book went on the same vein about the trip to the Canyon:

> . . . the traveler is carried through some of the most beautiful and diversified scenery of the Rockies. The drive is sixty-five miles long, which is easily accomplished in ten hours, there being four relays of horses for the journey, so that the animals are always fresh, and the road being a solid mountain free from any obstruction, jars and jolts are almost unknown. The course is along what is perhaps the most beautiful scenery in Arizona or elsewhere. For the first twenty miles it lies through a beautiful forest of pine trees, dotted here and there with parks, circling the base of the far-famed San Francisco Mountains, past pre-historic cave dwellings and away out into the open prairie, relieved by tracts of scrub cedar and pinyon trees, the home of the prairie-dog and antelope. An excellent lunch can be procured at Cedar Ranch, thirty-four miles from Flagstaff, and thence once more away across the prairie through

Cottonwood Canyon, where geologists can find much to interest them, one side of the canyon being about fifty feet wide, being composed of limestone formation while the opposite side is malapai. Then bounding over the prairie again until Moqui is reached, and a few miles further when the road again lies through the lordly Coconino Forest interspersed with sylvan glades and fragrant meadows for about twenty miles...

The flowery oratory of stagecoach hucksters promised—"a journey you'll never forget—" They were right. Most riders wouldn't forget the bruises for days to come. Indeed, inside the bounding stagecoach would be no place to host a tea party.

Remains of the Hance stage station at Grand Canyon just before demolition by the National Park Service. *(Photographer: David Eiting)*

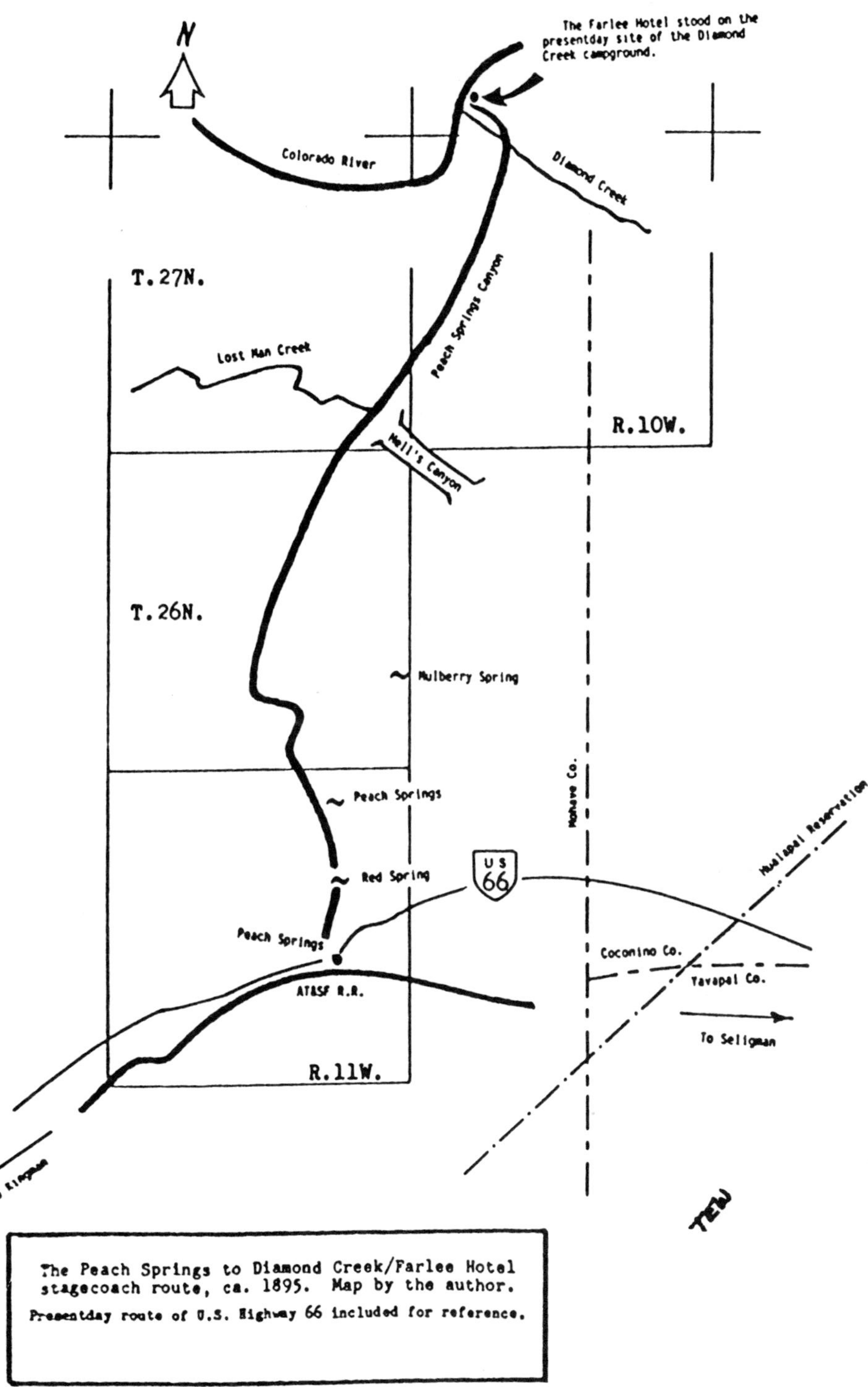

The Peach Springs to Diamond Creek/Farlee Hotel stagecoach route, ca. 1895. Map by the author.
Presentday route of U.S. Highway 66 included for reference.

John Verkamp, Sr., in front of his tent store at Grand Canyon in 1898. *(Photo courtesy of the Verkamp family)*

Automobiles

The transition from stagecoach to automobile was not immediate. After all, the horseless carriage was an untried mode of travel and if trouble developed on the trail, who knew how to fix a gasoline-motivated engine?

However, as time has a habit of periodically altering our habits, drivers were quick to acclimate themselves and learn the ways of the automobile. As one driver put it—"driving that auto is a big improvement over staring a string of horses in the butt all day."

What is purported to be the first automobile that ever attempted the journey to Grand Canyon was a Toledo six-wheel steamer. The anticipated 3½-hour journey required two days to complete.

Al Doyle, a name well known in Flagstaff circles, and three companions—Oliver Lippencott, T. M. Chapman, and W. C. Hoganboom, an editor of a Los Angeles paper—were the adventurers. That quartet left town in a bon voyage sendoff of well-wishers January 4, 1902.

The steam-powered car was considered the top of the line for automobiles. The solid rubber tires would preclude any tire trouble; more than fifty gallons of water was in the storage tank for the boiler. Almost the same amount of oil to heat the boiler was aboard.

A few miles from town, a faulty gasket in the steam gauge rendered that instrument useless, causing difficulty in keeping the steam at a steady pressure. The wrong type of oil was causing clouds of smoke to pour out of the firebox.

The party finally limped into a rancher's line shack where they spent the night.

The next morning they discovered the water in the boiler was frozen. When the water thawed enough to start the engine they found several leaks in the pipes caused by the freezing water. After a mile or two on a coughing engine the sprocket chain

Toledo steam car at Grand Canyon in 1902. This was the first automobile to reach the rim. *(Photographer unknown. Courtesy National Park Service, Grand Canyon National Park)*

broke, which spelled *finis* to any more use of the vehicle that day. A bitterly cold north wind added to the discomfort of the adventurers most of the day. Two of the party headed for Grandview afoot to find help which they found in the person of Pete Berry.

Late that night the venerable, but deposed, steamer finished the trip to Grandview, being towed by Pete Berry's team of horses. The steamer was said to have been repaired, and to make the trip "official" was finally nursed from Pete's place up to the rim, a few yards away, three days after it left Flagstaff.

The first automobiles to reach the North Rim were a Locomobile and a Thomas Flyer. They made the trip in 1909 from Kanab, Utah, in three days. These gasoline-powered cars had almost no engine trouble. They did, however, encounter other setbacks. Passengers had to make road repairs in several locations along the primitive trail. Tire troubles belabored the group; they wore out nine tires.

The debut performance of that old Toledo steamer on the scene started a new trend in transportation to the Canyon. But, it was a long time before there was any need of traffic control along the road. Technical science moved much faster on the improvement of the auto than it did on the road construction.

Travel to the Grand Canyon by automobile in 1918 was still a test of endurance, both for the vehicle and those who dared to make the trip. There was very little road, recognizable as such, just tracks in the ground where the few cars had been and the ruts where wheels had sunk into the mud during the rainy season.

During the summer of 1918 the author—then aged nine years—visited the Canyon with his family. Earlier that year Dad had bought a 1918 Dodge "touring car" and this was to be our

Pete Berry in front of his Flagstaff saloon. *(Courtesy National Park Service, Grand Canyon National Park)*

Saginaw-Manistee loader near Apex, 1930's. *(Photo courtesy Harry Matson, Williams)*

means of travel.

Dad had been talking to John H. Maxwell at the Saginaw & Manistee Lumber Company where both were employed and the two men discovered a common ambition. Both had recently arrived in Williams from elsewhere with their families. Both men had automobiles. Bobby Way owned the aforementioned Dodge and J. H. Maxwell owned a Model-T Ford. Both men wanted to see the Grand Canyon but neither wanted to attempt the trip alone.

On the supposition that the hazards of the road would be better surmounted by a group, the two decided to pool their resources and travel together. Accordingly, one day, well before the crack of dawn, the Maxwell and Way families loaded their respective cars with food, camping paraphernalia, gasoline and water for the journey and set out on the great adventure.

The first few miles out of Williams, the tracks were easy to follow as that section of road was in daily use by local ranchers. However, in some rocky areas farther along, we had to get out and search for the continuation of the so-called "highway."

We went through four rainstorms that day and with the coming of each downpour, we had to put up the side curtains and then take them down again after each deluge was over. Among other "joys of motoring, 1918-style," every time we put up the side curtains, we had to put the mud chains on the back wheels. Paved roads were a long time in the future and the mud chains were intended to provide increased traction on the muddy roads. Today's motorist uses the same chains on ice and snow in the winter. They are now known as "snow" chains. Way back when, the auto was not used during the winter in areas where it snowed. Old Betsy was put in a shelter out of the snowstorms; the car was jacked up and put on blocks or saw horses, or anything available; the tires were usually deflated; the radiator was drained; and the battery was taken into the house where it wouldn't freeze. The next spring, the motorist reversed the process to make the horseless carriage serviceable again.

Another hazard of our 1918 trip was rattlesnakes. These reptiles were scattered across the Coconino Plateau in great numbers and the majority seemed to be engaged in journeys of their own. It seems that these snakes live for a certain length of time in one area and then move on to a new locale when the pickings get slim around the rabbit or prairie dog burrows and packrat nests. Our own migration that day disrupted this scaley itinerary. We ran over seven of them on the way.

Another diversion was the frequent incidence of blowouts. We had seven or eight enroute and each one was cause for stopping the car, getting out, laboring with a hand jack, removing the flat tire, patching it with patches and implements from the tool kit without which no motoring trip was complete in those days, re-inflating the tire with an "Armstrong-powered" bicycle-type pump to a pressure of 65 pounds, replacing the tire, lowering the car, re-embarking the passengers and continuing on to the site of the next pit stop. Needless to say, the 64-mile trip took all of one summer's day, from much before dawn to well after dark.

We eventually pulled in and made camp where the Fred Harvey garage was later built. Owing to the lack of proper facilities, the Maxwells availed themselves of the nearness of the Bright Angel Lodge to book a room for their two daughters, Elsie and Helen. Once they were settled in, the elder Maxwells returned to the camp where the Way elders had just finished admonishing their children—"don't wander off and fall in the Canyon."

A locomotive whistle awakened us the next morning and in the light of day we discovered that we were only a short distance from the Santa Fe train depot in a hollow below the rim. Above the station on the rim itself stood the stately El Tovar Hotel. Farther west, the Bright Angel Lodge, from whence the Maxwell girls rejoined the rest of us for breakfast in due course, furnished the only other public accommodations at what is now Grand Canyon Village. This trip to the Canyon took place a year before the Grand Canyon became a National Park (February 26, 1919).

With the Grand Canyon becoming a national park, serious consideration was given to the building of a better highway, but it was still several years before a graded and adequately drained thoroughfare was completed.

In 1920, park records disclose, 50,075 train passengers visited Grand Canyon, compared with 10,260 who traveled by automobile. Train travel held its own until 1926, then fell rapidly behind. In 1950 only 48,097 passengers came by train, while well over 500,000 came by automobile.[9]

That pretty well places the time period when the wandering highway straightened out many of its kinks. It wasn't until the middle or late 1920s that the approach to Grand Canyon received a road worthy of the name. In many places the highway was graded and culverts were installed in most of the troublesome arroyos. Shortly thereafter the road was modernized by black-topping. The automobile then reigned supreme in the role of getting the Canyon within reach of the traveling public.

Railroads

First train carrying passengers to Grand Canyon, 1901. *(From the Leo Black collection)*

In 1886 interested Flagstaff citizens started a movement to construct a railroad from that town to Grand Canyon. The Flagstaff and Grand Canyon Railroad Company was formed.[10] A full slate of officers was elected, the president of which went east to solicit the money markets for the necessary funds for the project. He was unable to secure financial backing; most of those he contacted had never heard of the Grand Canyon, and some of them refused to believe there was such a fabulous canyon in the west.[11]

The Flagstaff and Grand Canyon Railroad Company was

dormant for almost three years. Then, in 1889 the Fifteenth Arizona Territorial Legislature enacted legislation[12]...

> That any corporation duly organized and incorporated under the laws of the Territory which shall construct a railroad from some point upon the line of the Atlantic & Pacific Railroad to some suitable point upon the Grand Canyon shall be exempted, and every species of property, real, personal and mixed, owned, held or used or occupied by said company for the purpose of constructing, operating and maintaining said road shall be exempt from taxation of every kind... during the process of construction and for the period of six years from and after completion of said railroad...this act shall not apply to any corporation which does not in good faith commence the construction of said railroad within two years of the passage of this act...

The Flagstaff Company reorganized and renewed their assault on eastern financial sources, but with no success.

Although the Atlantic & Pacific endorsed the stage line from Flagstaff to the Canyon, they offered no encouragement toward building a branch rail line. It would mean from eighty-five to ninety miles of track. They suggested a shorter route. Nothing further was done concerning a branch rail line to Grand Canyon until 1897.

Buckey O'Neill, Martin Buggeln, Sanford Rowe and John Verkamp, among others, often crossed paths and discussed the waste of scenery on the comparatively few people who saw the Canyon. Buggeln, having been a locomotive fireman, probably was the first to seriously suggest the feasibility of a railroad branch line. Passengers could be transported in greater comfort in less time; the mines could be profitably worked and the ore shipped to smelters. A railroad from the Atlantic & Pacific mainline in Williams, a distance of sixty miles, would soon be self-supporting.

The need for the railroad was two-fold: transportation of sightseers and hauling ore from the mines. Flagstaff, in their bid for the railroad, stressed only the hauling of passengers; the lack of interest in the importance of handling freight might have been their downfall. Cattle and sheep raising were growing industries along the route.

Loaded with all of this information, O'Neill jumped on the suggestions with both feet... He had many influential friends in the east who had money.

Williams, Arizona, prior to the fire of July 2, 1901. Engine #49 (right, foreground) saw service on the Grand Canyon run. *(Photo courtesy Santa Fe Railway)*

The going was rough. O'Neill haunted the offices of investment houses in New York. "Arizona is too far out in the boondocks to expect any financial help," seemed to be their universal answer to Buckey's pleas for financial backing.[13]

He backtracked to Chicago where he faced the same lack of enthusiasm from the Windy City's investment brokers. On the verge of failure—Buckey never gave up—he found a ray of light in the investment firm of Lombard, Goode & Company. They would, they said, send representatives, including a geologist and mining expert, to examine the possibilities of the proposed mining venture and its potential value to ensure a return on their proposed investment.

Buckey's joy knew no bounds. He arranged a date to meet the party at Flagstaff with the fanciest and sturdiest coach the stage line boasted.

Before dawn that morning the party left Flagstaff in a cloud of dust with Buckey driving the six-horse hitch; he was taking no chances. He promised not only to show them great copper deposits but scenery beyond anything they had ever seen.

As the coach bounced over the rocks and in and out of ruts, through clouds of choking dust, the patience of the guests wore thin. It took much earnest persuasion to convince the party they should continue on to the Canyon instead of turning back. Finally after eleven hours of almost continually grabbing something solid to hold onto inside the bounding stage, they arrived at their destination—Buckey's little two-room hotel. It was after dark on a moonless night.

Early the next morning the tired guests had their first glimpse of Grand Canyon. The bone-bruising stage trip was all but forgotten, but it had been a narrow squeak. Tempers had flared, but the Canyon seemed to hold a healing balm that soothed ruffled feelings and tired muscles.

Later that day, Buckey took his guests by stage to view some mining claims near Rowe's Well. The geologist used "fabulous," among other superlative terms, to describe his feelings concerning the value of the claims.

Buckey O'Neill extolled the virtues of the scenery, mining possibilities, health-giving quality of the air—everything he could think of to maintain the interest of his guests. When they returned to Chicago they were as enthused over the new venture as was Buckey.

Lombard, Goode & Co. wasted no time. They bought up every available mining claim in the area and mining machinery, destined for Grand Canyon, began to arrive in Flagstaff where it was transferred from the train to the beds of freight wagons for the final leg to the mines. Geologists combed the area in search of new ore deposits.

Hauling that heavy mining machinery by wagon did much to

Fray Marcos Hotel, Williams, date unknown. *(From a postcard in the author's collection)*

Locomotive in Flagstaff, Arizona. This engine saw service on the Williams-Grand Canyon line. Date unknown. *(Photo courtesy Williams News)*

encourage the construction of the branch line to connect with the main line of the Atlantic & Pacific in Williams. The principal investor, Lombard, Goode & Co., was deeply involved in the mining business. They had started initial exploratory operations and were buying up claims from Rowe's Well south to Anita, 11 miles distant. They would soon sink shafts and would then have an urgent need for a rail line on which to ship ore to a smelter. In anticipation of the latter, the company constructed a 50-ton smelter in Williams. The anticipation in that case was greater than the realization though as the smelter may have only processed a single ore shipment before it ceased operations for good. Some sources claim that the smelter never was used at all.

Anyway, Lombard, Goode & Co. contributed financial backing for the new railroad and urged private investors to do likewise. A few Williams businessmen did, including Frank Polson and his brother August (Gus) and George Young, publisher and editor of the ***Williams News***.[14]

The Atlantic & Pacific Railroad had expressed interest in the venture but the financial troubles which forced that entity into receivership in March, 1896, precluded any investment or assistance by them.[15] In May, 1897, the reorganized railroad company came back to life as the Santa Fe Pacific Railroad, pseudonym for the Atchison, Topeka and Santa Fe Railroad.

An early-day coal burner (Engine #83) in Williams, Arizona, yard. *(Photo courtesy Williams News)*

Buckey O'Neill was not around to see the branch line's completion. The excitement was over and the railroad assured. It was time to move on.

He sold his cabin and bunkhouse to Ralph Cameron, then sheriff of Coconino County. Cameron added these buildings to his newly-completed two-story Cameron Hotel nearby. He maintained this hotel property for several years and eventually it was sold to Fred Harvey.

Early in 1898 war clouds started gathering over Cuba. O'Neill went back to Prescott. He wanted to get in on the action, particularly after learning that his old friend, Teddy Roosevelt, was in charge of organizing a military unit called "Teddy's Terrors." They would later be known as the renowned Rough Riders.

Buckey didn't survive the trip to Cuba. A Spanish sniper's bullet caught up with him on Kettle Hill. He had, however, planted the seed; he had removed many obstacles from the path to expedite the establishment of the railroad to Grand Canyon.

Construction of the roadbed started in June 1899[16]. Early in 1900, when the rails had been laid to within eleven miles of their destination, Grand Canyon, work stopped. The mines had played out. The seemingly endless deposits of rich copper ore had merely been scattered pockets; though rich in content, they were too small to yield the hoped-for riches anticipated by the owners.

Lombard, Goode & Co., the majority investor, refused to invest further to complete the line. That left the small investors out on a limb. They had no choice but to sell at almost a total loss. There was no rolling stock—nothing but the uncompleted track and right-of-way. George U. Young, publisher-editor of the ***Williams News*** and an investor in the ill-fated rail venture, made a few choice remarks (and who could blame him?) in his paper—June 22, 1901,—

"Any fool can build a railroad, but it takes a wise man to be patient while the other fellow builds it then takes it away from him.

"With due respect to all courts and lawyers, Williams would have been a million dollars better off today if she had never heard of either. . . the Santa Fe out-bid everyone for the Grand Canyon Railroad. We bid. . . we bid. . . you all good day!"

On July 18, 1901, the sale was finalized and the Santa Fe became the owner of record of the Grand Canyon Railroad.[17] They had previously consolidated their efforts with those of the stage line and for more than 18 months, a combined train-stagecoach service had been offered to the public. Trains traversed the 55 miles of completed track and the stagecoaches completed the journey from "End-of-Track" to the Canyon, 11 miles away.

Early in the life of this odd co-partnership, tourist travel increased rapidly, due in great part to the advertising power of the Santa Fe system. Prior to Santa Fe's formal acquisition of the track, the tacit agreement between the two had worked well as Santa Fe trains had been using the track as early as mid-March or early April of 1900.[18]

A two-mile spur line ran from Anita Junction on the main line, to the mines at Anita. When these mines played out, the spur was abandoned and Anita Junction became Anita.

With what might have been a strained complacence, the ***Williams News*** of February 23, 1901 printed several items on the subject of travel to the Canyon:

> The Grand Canyon Railroad is proving itself to be 60 miles of as valuable railroad track as there is in the southwest and stands, as an investment, pre-eminently ahead and above most tracks of such length...

and,

> The first double-header passenger train over the Santa Fe & Grand Canyon Railroad started early Thursday morning (Feb. 21st). The train consisted of three magnificent special cars of the New York Central Railroad, a magnificent dining car of the Southwestern Limited, besides a baggage car. The train contained Dr. Webb, son-in-law of W. K. Vanderbilt, his family and a party of twelve friends. Engines 49 and 610, with engineers Schlee and Henderson at the throttles, made a pretty sight as they steamed across the plateau, pulling the magnificent train.
>
> Martin Buggeln, the liveryman, shipped all of his extra stages and carriages over the Santa Fe & Grand Canyon Railroad, Monday, to the end of the track. Several big excursions of tourists are on the road and conveyances already at the end of the track were not sufficient to take care of the travel. Consequently Mr. Thurber (Santa Fe transportation manager) had to call into requisition all the conveyances he could...

In the March 16, 1901 issue (business was still booming)...

> Bert Adams came in from the stage line at the end of the track to the Canyon Thursday, returning again yesterday. Active preparations are being made to handle the three special trains of tourists which will arrive today.
>
> Three or four years ago, when the ***News*** asserted that a railroad to the Grand Canyon would be an eight to ten percent proposition, the idea was scoffed at. The present is proving that that estimate was by no means sufficiently optimistic.

The Santa Fe completed the construction of track from Anita to the Grand Canyon, declaring that the line was "open for business" on July 1st, 1901.[19] On August 10th of that year, the purchasers incorporated under the name of the Grand Canyon Railway Company, a separately-operated but wholly-owned part of the Santa Fe system.

Shortly after the coming of the rails Fred Harvey, an eastern restaurateur who had been growing with the Santa Fe Railroad as it moved west, acquired interests at Grand Canyon. In addition to the Bright Angel Hotel, which he had bought before, Harvey installed a fleet of horse-drawn carriages to better serve

Surrey in front of El Tovar Hotel, 1910. *(From the collection of R. J. Connor, Jr., Williams, Arizona)*

passengers arriving on the trains.

In 1905 the El Tovar Hotel was opened by Harvey to add to his expanding empire. The fame of Grand Canyon then grew fast, its beauty far outshadowing the value of the forgotten, exhausted copper mines.

The day of the stagecoach was about over at Grand Canyon. Cap Hance had moved his residence to the blossoming new Grand Canyon Village, where he devoted his full attention to furthering the education (?) of gullible tourists with his far-out stories.

After the rail line was completed the stages were used on the rim drives, giving the travelers views of the Canyon from nearby points. Before long Fred Harvey bought out and/or usurped the franchise (if any existed) of the rim drives.

Buggeln still transported passengers to his hotel at Grandview from the Grand Canyon train terminal. In later years Harvey carriages added that route to their ever-expanding transportation system. They enjoyed the burgeoning tourist business as a result of the train's popularity as a means of travel. More miles of primitive roads were being constructed and existing roads improved along the rim for the enjoyment of the tourist. Coaches, other than Harvey-owned, were soon thereafter out of business.

A post office was established at Grand Canyon March 14, 1902, with Martin Buggeln being named postmaster.[20] A post office designated "Grandview," was again opened on November 27, 1903 at the Hance station at Grandview Point, in the same building that had previously been designated "Tourist." Harry H. Smith was named postmaster.[21] The life of this reborn renamed post office lasted five years,dying an ignominious death on November 30, 1908.[22]

The Hance and Buggeln properties were later acquired by William Randolph Hearst, who built an elaborate cabin near the Canyon rim. The National Park Service eventually obtained title to the Grandview property and restored it to public domain. In the progression of Park Service policy these old landmarks have long since been demolished; they apparently interfered with the natural beauty of the surroundings.

Railroading on the Grand Canyon Line was not without certain perils in its early-day operation. The right-of-way was unfenced and consequently many forms of livestock fell victim to the trains. Horses, cattle, sheep, burros, etc., all suffered heavy losses in encounters with the steam locomotives in right-of-way arguments. An occasional deer was killed, but wild animals seemed to learn more quickly to not argue with the steel monsters. Domestic animals never learned and for many years it was a rare occasion when a train made the Canyon run, after dark, without hitting at least one animal.

Engine crews were fast to take protective action. When the headlight picked out an animal on or near the tracks, the crew quickly closed their windows, if time permitted, and jumped from their seats to the protection offered behind the boiler and hoped for the best. If they were not quick enough, various parts of the animal might wind up in their laps. One hoghead (engineer) stated—"It was always messy, especially when we got the 'used grass' from a cow plastered all over us, and the engine heat heightened the smell. We couldn't stop—we didn't have time—besides, an emergency stop would throw passengers around causing injuries . . ."

This "two-spot" locomotive of ALT (previously Saginaw/Manistee) was used at Apex. *(Photo by the author in Flagstaff, ca. 1979-80)*

The railroad found it much less expensive to pay the stockmen for their losses than to fence the right-of-way. An excitable engineer could make an emergency stop and cause many injuries to passengers. It was far less hazardous and less expensive to keep the train moving, unless it happened to be moving at a slow speed whereby a stop could be made in safety to the passengers.

Of all animals, sheep were the most feared by trainmen. Though smaller than many other species of livestock, an engineer would rather hit an elephant than a sheep. The wool and tallow of a sheep would ball-up under the wheels and undercarriage and foul up the air lines to the brakes and very often cause a derailment. Running into a band of sheep could create havoc and always meant serious trouble.

When an animal was hit, a report was made to the nearest section maintenance crew. They, in turn, were required to clear and maintain the track and right-of-way. In addition to their extra pay (it was nearly always nighttime and consequently off-duty hours), they salvaged all edible meat for their own use. It was said the Santa Fe had a well-fed group of section crews, both on the Canyon line and the mainline.

Grand Canyon Railway depot, circa 1975-80). *(Photo courtesy Santa Fe Railway)*

Shortly after the inception of this branch line, the Santa Fe adopted a regular schedule for their Pullman service. The *California Limited*, one of their top through trains from Chicago to the West Coast, arrived in Williams at 10:43 p.m. each night. The Pullman cars containing those passengers who were scheduled for the Canyon trip were taken from the *Limited* and switched to the Canyon siding. The cars from the previous night's train were switched onto the *Limited*, which continued on to the West Coast. Many passengers slept through the entire procedure.

An item in an early-day brochure, extolling the virtues of rail travel to the Canyon, stated succinctly—"Ride in comfort in our modern coaches and arrive at Grand Canyon relaxed and ready to enjoy the most scenic area in the world."

The Canyon train containing the Pullman cars switched from the *California Limited* left Williams at 5:30 a.m., arriving at Grand Canyon at 6:50. The return trip was begun at 8:40 p.m.

and reached Williams at 10 o'clock, having allowed the passengers a full day to enjoy the Canyon. For many years the *California Limited* and the Grand Canyon line performed this popular daily service that began in November, 1904. For two years before that, it was a semi-weekly service of trains leaving Chicago on Tuesdays and Saturdays.

In later years another regularly-scheduled train made a daily trip from Los Angeles to Grand Canyon. This train picked up a Pullman car set off in the Williams yard by the *San Francisco Chief* and took it to and from the Canyon. The car was then picked up by the next *San Francisco Chief* and continued its mainline journey.

In the heyday of Pullman travel (1920's up into the '50's) it was not unusual to see three, four or more sections of an extra train at one time at Grand Canyon. The section, although a complete train in itself, was a part of and traveled under the number assigned the extra train. Often an entire train was required to accommodate traveling royalty and their entourages from foreign countries. Special excursions of conventioneers added this side trip to their itineraries either on the way to or from their respective conventions. Specials of one sort or another were an almost daily occurrence.

The Fred Harvey pavilions of refreshment and repose—El Tovar and Bright Angel hotels and dining rooms—were oftimes taxed to the limit by the influx of sight-seers. Although the Pullmans were homes away from home, not everyone came by Pullman. Some came by chair car and automobile and needed hotel accommodations.

Another daily train to the Canyon left Williams about noon and returned about 7 p.m. This train usually consisted of one chair car and one combination chair and baggage-mail car. The chair car had an observation deck on the back end. This train operated on a "local" schedule, making several stops to deliver mail. Ranchers out along the line received their mail at Williams but rarely came to town. To take care of this situation the mail clerk delivered the mail along the route, where feasible.

The combination baggageman-mail clerk was also a Samaritan of sorts. Often, before the train was due to leave, orders of groceries and other commodities in cartons from Babbitt-Polson and/or Duffy Brothers were delivered to the baggage car. The consignee was at some specified point along the track to meet the train. A stop was nearly always made at Valle and Anita. Before starting out, the clerk advised the engineer of the various stops to make and away they went.

Sometimes the mail clerk was the only person a lonesome cowboy or sheepherder spoke to for weeks at a time. At Anita, Yeager-Bly Cattle and Sheep Company had a mail-grocery drop. They had built a pack rat and coyote-proof perch near the livestock loading chute close to the tracks. If nobody was there to meet the train, the supplies and mail were left on that tamper-proof (from marauding animals) perch.

The Saginaw & Manistee Lumber Company in Williams logged the Skinner Ridge area in the late 1920's and early '30's. Their logging equipment brought the loaded cars to Apex where the Santa Fe coupled on and brought the logs to the Saginaw sawmill in Williams. This logging operation covered the Skinner Ridge area, now known as the Tusayan District, adjacent to the south boundary of the Grand Canyon National Park.

Saginaw-Manistee loader near Flagstaff, circa 1915. This equipment later moved to Apex. *(Photo courtesy Harry Matson, Williams, Arizona)*

Fray Marcos Hotel and Red Cross Canteen, Williams, Arizona, in the 1940's. *(From a postcard in the author's collection)*

Northern Arizona was buffeted by an unusually heavy snowfall in the winter of 1948-49. Highways to and from Grand Canyon were closed in. Ranchers were accommodated by the obliging railroad personnel who hauled food for them and their families and hay for their snowbound livestock. One engineer reminisced—"you could see smoke and fires close to the track long before we got there—there'd have been a lot of people and stock lost that winter if we hadn't come along—the people might have managed somehow or other to have gotten out, but I'm sure we saved a lot of stock."

Freight service was maintained on a regular schedule. Three freight trains a week were scheduled except when cattle and sheep were shipped, then the line was busy day and night throughout the shipping season. Sheep particularly were a large item in keeping business booming for the railroad. The woolies were shipped south to a lower pasture for the winter months, then brought back for the summer season to the higher range after lambing.

By this time, the automobile and truck were making inroads into the travel and freight market and business, both passenger and freight, fell off and became uncertain. Regular passenger service over the Grand Canyon line was replaced by motor coach shuttle in September, 1967,[23] and by mid-1969, even the sporadic freight service stopped altogether. Even the area stockmen found it more convenient to ship by truck.

History repeats itself, although the process is sometimes long and the pitfalls are numerous. The possibility of the Grand Canyon Line being reopened again would hover over the once-busy rails for twenty years before the reincarnated rail line returned to life.

During the inactive period many attempts were made to reactivate the venerable old line. They all made serious attempts to revitalize the project; some of the hastily-formed organizations had incorporated in their zeal to put new life into the old line.

An old legend in the archives of railroading has it that an Irish hoghead named Finnegan had trouble keeping his train on the tracks of a mythical railroad. Each time he was plagued with a derailment his reports to headquarters were long and filled with useless information. Headquarters had told him repeatedly to shorten his reports and "leave out the blarney!" Following his next derailment he sent in the following meager message—"Off Again—On Again—Gone Again—Finnegan."

Feasibility of the Grand Canyon Line was established by the Arizona Department of Transportation but, unlike Finnegan, none of the "railroad organizers" got the line going again.

The National Park Service expressed concern over the parking problem for automobiles at the Canyon. Each time the rumblings of rumor concerning the reviving of the line were heard, the Park Service lent an attentive ear. In recent years automobile traffic to the Canyon had increased so rapidly a two-fold obstacle was being created—parking space was at a premium and the vastly increased number of vehicles had stimulated what could soon become a smog problem.

Grand Canyon has been described as being one of the last places in the country where one may still breathe smog-free air. The Park Service would like to maintain that environment intact. Less auto traffic at and around the park would be a step in the right direction. Tourists could ease the problem by leaving their vehicles in Williams and using the train facilities. The route

Pre-inaugural run of Grand Canyon Railway leaving Sweetwood Crossing on 9/17/89. Smoke from the steam engine is visible in the distance at rear of the train in foreground of the picture. *(Photo by the author)*

is scenic to some degree but its main interest lies in its historic scope. People might enjoy a trip on this standard-gauge train back into the unhurried atmosphere of yesteryear's steam-powered railroad transportation.

Since the untimely demise of train travel on the Grand Canyon line more than two decades past—the tracks remained in place. Vandalism and lack of maintenance took their toll, but the line was not completely beyond repair.

Throughout those twenty years, the thought was nurtured by many that somehow, the old Grand Canyon line might again blossom into a new existence. However, each time that interest was aroused, the same obstacle would eventually spread a wet blanket over the plans—MONEY—lots of money was needed. In 1901, the Santa Fe Railroad had surmounted the obstacle and pulled that chestnut out of the fire but, nearly ninety years later, that sort of ready salvation for the line was no longer a possibility. What was needed was a company which could combine the know-how of railroad operation with adequate financing to accomplish the feat. In due course, such an entity appeared on the scene as the new Grand Canyon Railway.

The new railway is under the leadership of businessman Max Biegert, who is chairman and chief executive officer. Biegert's wife, Thelma, is secretary and treasurer; Robert L. Roth is president and chief operations officer; and Brian K. Alexander is vice president of railroad operations.

The company also plans a 20-year program of construction and development, including a motel and restaurant complex and a theme park to complement the railroad operation.

Steam-operated locomotives again sing the song of the rails and clicking switches as they pull the vintage cars over the route. Antiquated old-style cars that once traveled the rails have been taken out of the moth balls and renovated. Steam locomotives that once furnished the power again reign over the Grand Canyon Railway.

A pre-inaugural run September 17, 1989, commemorated the original inaugural of 1901. Following dedication ceremonies, the trains operated on special occasions through the fall months, including Saturdays, Sundays and holidays, and a

Locomotive #18, purchased by the Grand Canyon Railway for use on the new Williams-Grand Canyon run, 1989. *(Courtesy the H. K. Vollrath Collection and the Grand Canyon Railway)*

regular daily schedule began in early Spring, 1990.

This new railway venture was not without its share of trials and tribulations. Most of those whose advice would have been invaluable have long since passed from the scene and many of the still-extant operational records are widely scattered.

During most of the night preceding the "pre-inaugural" run, Locomotive #18 (a vintage ALCO 2-8-0 Consolidated) was being worked on and tested for its grand entrance the next day. Some adjustment was necessary. The engine had not been used for some years prior to its purchase by the Grand Canyon Railway, and the run to the Canyon includes mountain grades, a great difference from the engine's previous workplace on the shores of Lake Superior, where the ground is mostly level.

The pre-inaugural run got off to a somewhat late start on September 17, 1989. Amid the cheers of a large and enthusiastic crowd and many blasts of its steam whistle, the train started on its run from the Williams depot under a huge plume of black smoke. Behind the locomotive and tender there were seven passenger cars and, bringing up the rear, the Railway's two diesel engines. These diesels saved the day as they nudged the train from the rear over the course of its run to Grand Canyon depot, the site of another inaugural ceremony later in the day. The revered old #18 didn't make the return trip that day. It was uncoupled and left at Grand Canyon overnight while the coaches made the return pulled by the diesels.

Not only did the new railroaders roll back the pages of history that day, they even managed to provide a taste of a few historical hardships enroute. Through it all, however, the long-sought steam train has once again begun running to the Grand Canyon.

Notes

1. Fuchs, James R. "A History of Williams, Arizona, 1976-1951." ***Social Science Bulletin 23, U of A Bulletin,*** Vol. XXIV, No. 5 (Nov. 1953). Page 77.
2. A telephone conversation with Mr. and Mrs. William Bass, son and daughter-in-law of W. W. Bass and correspondence with Stephen G. Maurer of Heritage Associates, Albuquerque, NM; both in the course of research for the first edition in 1980.
3. As above. Also, a reference in the ***Coconino Sun*** of Sept. 5, 1891.
4. ***Coconino Sun***, September 19, 1892.
5. Theobald, John O. and Lillian Theobald. ***Arizona Territory: Post Offices and Postmasters***. AHF, Phoenix. 1961. Page 132.
6. *Ibid.* Page 132.
7. Verkamp, Margaret M. ***History of Grand Canyon National Park***. Unpublished MA Thesis. U of A, Tucson. 1940. Page 40.
8. Keithley, Ralph. ***Buckey O'Neill.*** The Caxton Printers, Ltd. Caldwell, Idaho. 1949. Pages 202-203.
9. Fuchs. "A History of Williams, Arizona..." Page 160, Appendix 'E.'
10. Cline, Platt. ***They Came to the Mountain.*** NAU & Northland Press, Flagstaff. 1976. Page 204.
11. In Keithley's ***Buckey O'Neill,*** the story is recounted on pp. 204-206 about O'Neill driving a set of eastern investors to the rim of the Canyon. One was so overcome with the beauty of the site that he promised O'Neill any amount of money he wanted, just as long as he was left to admire the view unmolested...at least according to the story.
12. ***Arizona Weekly Miner***. Prescott, A. T. (April 15, 1895). This act is also quoted in Verkamp's ***History of Grand Canyon National Park*** on pp. 22-23. Source for the latter was ***Session Laws of the 15th Legislative Assembly of the Territory of Arizona.*** Act 28, pp. 37-38.
13. Keithley. ***Buckey O'Neill.*** page 202.
14. Fuchs. page 78.
15. Fuchs. page 66.
16. ***Coconino Sun***. (June 24, 1899). Quoted in Fuchs, page 78.
17. Fuchs. page 79.

18. A train/stagecoach schedule, with times effective March 15, 1900, was published in the ***Williams News*** of April 6, 1901, indicating that the combined service was available to S.F. & G.C. RR patrons at least by early April 1900.
19. Correspondence from the Public Relations department of Santa Fe Pacific Corporation says: "Our records indicate that the line was 'opened for business' on July 1, 1901." (Letter from Robert E. Gehrt, V.P., Public Relations to the author, dated November 22, 1989.)
20. Theobald. ***Arizona Territory: Post Offices and Postmasters***. page 103.
21. Theobald. page 103.
22. Ibid. page 103.
23. Passenger timetables for "Spring/Summer, 1967" state that train service would be in effect through Sept. 23, 1967 and that after that there would be motor coach service instead. While this was a "seasonal" notice, examination of timetables for February and August, 1968 both show motor coach service in lieu of train service. This indicates that the last regularly-scheduled passenger train ran on September 23, 1967. It is possible that some special trains ran after that date but there is no way of verifying this. Data from the Robert Gehrt letter of November 22, 1989.

Pre-inaugural run of Grand Canyon Railway approaching Sweetwood Crossing, about four miles north of Williams on September 17, 1989. *(Photo by the author)*

geles,
ı the
Cali-
ty of

posed
l the
rmed

e, or
nain-
spose
aphic
lines,
ıents,
per-
ness;
aphic
con-
e and
ıonic,
o re-
and
lly to
and
, and
ıeral
var-
ntain
tween
else-
con-
sub-
s, and
offices
aphic

e, or
ower,
d dis-
light,
ıereof
sub-
age in
heat

create
motor
appli-
kind
ise ac-
and to
g and

rights
pur-
rnish-
light,
struc-
phone
les.
perate
, man-
evices
nt for

erwise
l pur
intain

Not. Pub. Seal. W. F. BLAKE.

Williams News, April 6, 1901

Int. Rev. 10c. Cancelled.

Recorded Feb. 26, A. D., 1901, at 11:45 p. m., in Book 1, Articles of Incorporation, pages 328, 329, 330, 331 and 332, Records of Coconino County, Arizona.

H. C. HIBBEN, County Recorder.

First publication March 2, 1901.

Santa Fe & Grand Canyon R. R.

TIME CARD.

No. 10.	Miles	March 15, 1900.	No. 11.
P. M.			P. M.
12:30	0	Lv.....WILLIAMS.....Ar	6:30
1:00	9	.......RED LAKE.......	6:00
1:35	20	..........PRADO..........	5:30
2:00	29	..........VALLE..........	5:00
2:30	38	........WILLAHA........	4:30
3:00	45	...ANITA JUNCTION...	4:00
3:15	47	..........ANITA..........	3:45
		STAGE	
4:30	55	........COCONINO........	2:30
6:00	67	Ar..GRAND CANYON.Lv	1:30
P. M.			P. M.

HENRY F. ASHURST, ATTORNEY-AT-LAW
Practice in all Courts. Williams, Arizona.

Santa Fe Route TIME TABLE.

CORRECTED TO DECEMBER 27, 1900

No. 7.	No. 3.	No. 1.	STATIONS	No. 2.	No. 4.	No. 8
2 43 a	1 00 p	10 00 p	Leave .... Chicago .... Leave	7 40 a	2 15 p	9 00
2 30 a	2 20 a	10 55 a	.... Kansas City	5 45 p	2 40 a	8 00
	8 30 a	3 20 a	.... Denver	10 00 a	6 00 p	6 00
7 40 a	3 53 p	4 25 a	.... La Junta	10 30 p	11 52 a	9 45
10 00 p	4 10 a	7 00 p	...............Albuquerque...............	8 30 a	11 50 p	7 10
		2 25 a	...............Wingate...............	3 23 a		
4 00 a	9 25 a	2 15 a	...............Gallup....*...............	3 00 a	6 55 p	1 25
		5 45 a	...............Holbrook...............	11 35 p		
7 55 a	12 35 p	7 05 a	...............*..Winslow ..*...............	10 40 p	3 10 p	8 55
10 30 a	3 05 p	9 30 a	...............Flagstaff...............	8 42 p	1 25 p	6 40
12 05 p	4 25 p	11 12 a	...............Williams...............	7 18 p	12 10 p	5 15
1 05 p	5 25 p	12 10 p	...............*..Ash Fork...............	5 25 p	10 55 a	3 55
		6 00 p	...............Ash Fork...............	5 15 p		
			...............Jerome Junct...............	3 25 p		
		7 50 p	...............Jerome...............	10 45 a		
			...............Jerome Junct...............			
		8 45 p	...............Prescott...............	2 45 p		
		11 25 p	...............Congress Junction...............	11 19 a		
		2 35 a	...............Phoenix...............	8 45 a		
1 30 p		12 35 p	...............Ash Fork...............	5 50 p		3 55
		2 25 p	...............Peach Springs...............	1 45 p		12 20
4 15 p	8 05 p	3 55 p	...............Kingman...............	11 10 a	6 15 a	9 58
6 35 p	9 50 p	6 45 p	...............*.The Needles...............	8 20 a	4 00 a	7 00
8 00 p		8 10 p	...............Blake...............	7 05 a		5 45
		9 10 p	...............Bagdad...............	4 19 a		
		12 12 a	...............Daggett...............	2 25 a		
12 35 a	3 55 a	12 45 a	...............Barstow ...*...............	2 10 a	10 40 p	1 20
1 25 a		1 45 a	...............Kramer...............	1 05a		12 04
2 25 a		2 40 a	...............Mojave...............	12 15 a		11 10
	8 30 a	7 00 a	...............Los Angeles...............	7 15 p	6 00 p	
	12 45 p	12 45 p	...............San Diego...............	1 55 p	1 50 p	
2 25 a	5 40 a		...............Mojave...............		8 45 a	11 10
6 05 a	9 10 a		...............Bakersfield...............		5 30 a	7 40
10 30 a	11 50 a		...............Fresno...............		2 40 p	3 15
2 30 p	3 00 p		...............Stockton...............		11 50 a	11 10
5 55 p	5 55 p		...............San Francisco...............		9 00 a	8 00

J. J. BYRNE. G. P. A., Los Angeles, Cal N. J. HUDSON, Agent, Williams, Ari

Airplanes

Air travel to Grand Canyon had a meager beginning in the late 1920s. This method of travel was not immediately popular with the public. Most people were reluctant to get both feet that far off the ground at the same time. That apprehension would change but it was still several years before air travel enjoyed the popularity it has today.

The original Grand Canyon Airport was under the management of the Hudgins Air Service, headquartered at Tucson. The airport was located near the north slope of Red Butte, about eighteen miles by road from Grand Canyon Village.

There were no underground facilities for storage of gasoline, which was trucked in from Williams and stored in metal barrels. (AUTHOR'S NOTE: I drove that truck for Union Oil Company for a time in 1930.) Scenic flights over the Canyon emanated from this airport. In the beginning the airplane on the line had room for five passengers and the pilot. As airplanes became larger, runways, of necessity, became longer and this airport was outgrown. During this period Transcontinental and Western Air (the original TWA) made flag stops and later regular stops at the U.S. Government-operated airport at Valle, half-way between Williams and Grand Canyon. Incoming passengers were met by Fred Harvey bus and limousine services for the thirty-mile ride from there to the Canyon.

Present-day Grand Canyon Airport, six miles from the Canyon, can accommodate the largest airliners. Everything is modern except—well—what do you know? There, amid the myriad and varied array of modern aircraft, sits a Ford Tri-Motor airplane, a flash-back to the late 1920s, and as this is written, this venerable old airliner, on special occasions, still takes passengers out over the Canyon with that same slow celerity that gives one a good look at the scenery that was once seen only after a long and arduous journey by stagecoach and then only a horizontal glimpse.

This Ford tri-motor plane caused quite a stir in northern Arizona. *(Photo courtesy Smithsonian Institution, Washington, DC)*

Many travelers now visit the Canyon from afar by airplane, both private and commercial. According to Grand Canyon Airport figures, 450,074 tourists came by air in 1987 to see the Canyon on regularly-scheduled commercial flights. Of the several million tourists who visit the Grand Canyon each year, a fair percentage—in fact, a "lion's share," are transported by the airlines from all over the world.

Look closely as your plane glides into this modern airport. See that wisp of dust over there among the trees to your left? That could be a late-running stagecoach. Look closer. That could be Old "Cap" Hance up there hunkered over the seat, urging his six-horse hitch to put out a little more effort. As his unkempt beard flows back in your slipstream, you get a little better look at him—his mouth is going. Listen closer. . . that's it. . . he's telling a story about his famous horse, Babe (the animal had a different name nearly every time he told a story about it, and that was often). It seems like this horse, among its unlimited other accomplishments, could jump across Grand Canyon in one big leap. . . anyway. . .

"One day that rascal wasn't feelin' quite up to snuff. He took a short run and a half-hearted jump from the rim. Well sir, about halfway acrost, he saw he wasn't a'going to make 'er, so. . . did he give up and drop in the Canyon? Naw sir! not that beautiful hunk of hossflesh. He turned around and come back. . . took a longer run at it and that time he made 'er with room to spare. Fourteen mile jump it was. . . then, there was the other time. . . lemme see. . . back in 1889, it was. . ."

Beginning of a trail ride on March 5, 1946. Mrs. Raye Way, the author's wife, is directly behind the guide. *(Photo by Kolb Bros. Studio, Grand Canyon)*

The North Rim

The Canyon's scenic splendors, as seen from the North Rim, were hardly known or appreciated by the general public until recently, although many who have made the comparison declare that views from here, perhaps on account of the greater elevation, clearer air or comparative lack of manmade clutter as a distraction, are superior to those viewed from the South Rim. Be that as it may, the development of tourist facilities here has been slow.

The North Rim's climate, which because of the greater elevation (1,000 to 1,500 feet higher on the average), is cooler and wetter than that of the South Rim, reduces the length of the tourist season to only four or five months out of the year. The snows come earlier here and last longer. The surrounding country is rugged and sparsely populated and many of the roads that do exist are closed in winter. Highway construction was not a real priority until recently and the small population and difficulties of supply meant that airport construction of a size and scope sufficient to the requirements of today's airliners and commuter aircraft was not economically feasible. Since access to the area was so limited of possibility and difficult of accomplishment, only a fraction of the total number of park visitors over the years have made it to the North Rim to sample the cornucopia of natural wonders, not all of them geological.

The rugged terrain and isolation are ideal for big game and herds of elk and deer can often be seen from the roads. Outside of the National Park, the area is a hunter's paradise whose fame goes back long before the lion hunts of Teddy Roosevelt and "Uncle Jim" Owens at the turn of the century and to this day, trophy-sized trout still await the angler who painstakingly makes his way to the mouth of Thunder River, near where it empties into the Colorado.

In fact, it must have been the need to hunt for food that

brought the first prehistoric Indians to the North Rim. Game abounded there but the long cold winters and heavy snows probably ruled out year-round habitation and the area must have only been visited intermittently by migratory bands during the warmer months as the centuries and millenia slipped by.

While the dawn of a new era on the South Rim was heralded by the 1540 visit of Cardenas, his *conquistadores* and several taciturn Hopi guides, there is no definite record of when the first non-Indian stepped up to the edge of the chasm and gazed across the several intervening leagues from the other side. Coronado's other exploring detachments missed the North Rim country entirely and nearly 60 years later, Onate's party seems to have passed well to the south of even the South Rim on its 1598 trek to the mouth of the Colorado.

Since Spanish exploration was not usually undertaken for sightseeing or aesthetic purposes, and since Coronado's chroniclers had mentioned the arid nature of the territory and the fact that the great gorge was an impediment to travel, it may well have been that the later Spanish explorers consciously avoided the whole area as an obstacle in their quest for an overland route from the outposts of New Mexico to the settlements of Upper California.

Francisco Garces, as has already been mentioned, explored the Grand Canyon in 1776, but he did not cross over to the North Rim. However, during that same year, two of Garces' Franciscan proteges made a tentative entry into what is now called the "Arizona Strip"—without, however, reaching the North Rim. While Garces was visiting the Havasupai and the Hualapai, Fray Silvestre Escalante and Fray Francisco Dominguez, accompanied by a small escort of soldiers and packers, left Santa Fe on an exploratory trek to Monterey. After passing through what is now Colorado and Utah, the party had to turn back on account of bad weather and supply shortages. Entering presentday Arizona just south of St. George, the party headed back east, managing on the way to discover a crossing of the Colorado River in Glen Canyon.[1] Judging from the details of Fray Escalante's journal and the notations on a map prepared by one of the soldiers, it seems

Buffalo herd in House Rock Valley, circa 1930.
(Photo by the author)

unlikely that the group ever got as far as the North Rim; although they may have gotten as far south as the presentday course of the US89A highway through House Rock Valley. The first white man to see the Canyon from the North Rim probably happened along later, a generation after the end of Spanish sovereignty in the Southwest.

Not long after 1821, when the Mexican tricolor replaced the crimson and gold standard of Spain over the Governor's Palace in Santa Fe, a new kind of white man appeared in the wilderness and it was probably one of these who was the first non-Indian to step out to the edge of what is now Point Imperial or Cape Royal and stand open-mouthed in wonder. Whoever he was, he left no written record which might have inspired others to come and visit. Those kindred spirits who heard the stories by word-of-mouth in the decades that followed and made the journey were few and far between. The Mormons, moving south from Utah in the years after the Civil War, generally kept well away from the actual rim area as they founded their settlements in the Arizona Strip[2] and the Little Colorado Valley.

John Wesley Powell visited the North Rim, but even his glowing descriptions failed to trigger an avalanche of sightseers as the nineteenth century ended and the twentieth century began. The area was just too remote and hard to get to to interest anyone but an avid outdoorsman or conservationist. Coincidentally, at the beginning of the 20th Century, there was one of the latter in the White House.

In 1906, President Theodore Roosevelt established the Grand Canyon National Game Preserve on the Kaibab Plateau. Not only would this area be a home for the wild animals already there, it would be the site of a breeding experiment in which the famous hunter Charles J. "Buffalo" Jones attempted to cross domestic cattle with wild buffalo. The offspring would, it was hoped, combine the best traits of both parents and revolutionize the cattle industry. Unfortunately, the plan didn't quite come up to expectations. Perhaps the idea was ahead of its time but, after the few live births of a hybrid that was so depressingly ugly and puny that no one wanted to look at one, much less take it to market, the experiment quietly fizzled out. In 1928, Jones sold the remaining buffalo to the State of Arizona and this herd now ranges in House Rock Valley.[3]

Meanwhile, the Grand Canyon itself had become, by turns, a National Monument and a National Park. Visitors to the North Rim were still at a premium though and while the facilities at the South Rim constantly expanded to keep up with the increasing influx of visitors, the North Rim remained in nearly a pristine and primeval condition. But, this was about to change.

In 1926, a group of high school-age hikers, including the author, emerged at the trailhead on Bright Angel Point after a cross-canyon trek to find a wilderness but little changed from that which had greeted the Indians and the mountain men. From Thunder River on the west to Cape Royal on the east,

Louis Boucher leading a trail ride, date unknown. *(Courtesy National Park Service, Grand Canyon National Park)*

there was an unbroken forest, unmarked except for a few rough trails leading away towards the north and "civilization" at Fredonia. The only structure was a trailhead corral, built to contain the horses and mules belonging to the Forest Service and Fred Harvey and that, as I recall, was empty.

As things turned out though, our group may have presaged the coming of a new era as had Cardena's group on the other rim several centuries before. Construction soon began on the North Rim's first hotel.

In 1928, the Union Pacific Railroad got into the hotel business when it constructed the Grand Canyon Lodge on the North Rim. This building was destroyed by fire but was later rebuilt in its present form in 1936. This hotel is the only accommodation of this type inside the park and features a variety of different lodgings, from rustic cabins to modern motel units. The Grand Canyon Lodge is only open from mid-May to mid-October and the same holds true for the North Rim Campground, 1½ miles north of the lodge. Outside the park are the Kaibab Lodge, 18½ miles north of Bright Angel Point, open from June to September; and the Jacob Lake Inn, 45 miles north of the rim at Jacob Lake; as well as several campgrounds.

For years, the only way to get to the North Rim from the South Rim was by the roundabout 215-mile motor route east on State Route 64 to Cameron, north on US89, across to Jacob Lake on US89 Alternate via Marble Canyon and House Rock and then south to the park entrance on State Route 67 (lately designated a "State Scenic Parkway"). Needless to say, this discouraged quite a few would-be visitors and Grand Canyon Airways filled a longfelt need when it started daily runs to the North Rim from its terminal at Grand Canyon Airport during the May-to-October season some years ago. Also, and very recently, a shuttle service for aspiring North Rim visitors has been inaugurated from Grand Canyon Village. South Rim visitors can let someone else do the driving on the roundtrip daily runs as they take in the scenery. Information about this last service should be available at the Visitor's Center on the South Rim.

NOTES

1. This crossing became known to later generations of travelers as *el Vado de los Padres* (the Crossing of the Fathers). It has since been submerged by Lake Powell and lies under the waters of today's Padre Bay.

2. The Arizona Strip is that part of the state lying between the North Rim of the Grand Canyon and the Utah border.

3. House Rock Valley is east of Jacob Lake and the descendants of Buffalo Jones' breeding herd live here on a reserve established in 1951 by the Forest Service. The herd is controlled by the state Game and Fish Commission.

The Inner-Canyon Trails

So far, this narrative has dealt with travel *to* the Grand Canyon, but, from an early date there was a parallel and no-less-interesting saga being enacted below the rim as the presentday network of inner-canyon trails gradually took shape.

All of the trails within the national park are the responsibility of the National Park Service which supervises their use and maintenance. The degree of maintenance varies, though. The more traveled routes like the Bright Angel are well-maintained and boast such amenities as rest stations and campgrounds along their courses, while other, less well known historical routes like the "Old" Hance Trail have been allowed to revert almost to their primeval state.

In the early days, a variety of draft and riding animals were in use around the Canyon, but now the equine traffic below the rim is restricted to mules and an occasional horse. The Fred Harvey Company is the exclusive concessionaire for the inner-canyon mule trips and reservations for these unique excursions are often booked far in advance. In 1988, the collective long-eared membership of the Fred Harvey "taxi fleet" carried nearly 9,000 tourist riders through the Canyon on outings of varying distance and duration.* Privately-owned horses, while less common nowadays, may be ridden within the park and into the Canyon under the same general restrictions which apply to hikers[1] and in recent years, several stables offering rim rides and cross-country tours on rented animals have been in operation.

Hiking, which was the original means of descent into the Canyon, remains a popular means of seeing the sights. Each year, thousands of hikers leave the various trailheads headed into the depths of the gorge. While many content themselves with day trips, others set out on rim-to-rim treks taking several

*In 1988, 8980 people took mule rides at the Grand Canyon. Of these, 5103 took the one-day rides to Plateau Point and 3877 made the overnight trip to Phantom Ranch. Statistics courtesy: Grand Canyon National Park Lodges.

Hikers pose on inner-canyon suspension bridge across Colorado River near Bright Angel Creek in 1926. Author is at extreme left wearing hat. *(From the author's collection)*

days. While there are few restrictions on day hikers, a permit must be secured from the Backcountry Reservation Office for overnight hikes. Some people prefer the services of a guide on their hikes and a service has recently been created to meet that need.[2]

However the tourist of today proceeds, he or she invariably follows in the footsteps of those who went before on a network of trails, many of which date from a remote antiquity and were only developed to their present states fairly recently for reasons which had little or nothing to do with the Canyon's tourist industry.

The first human visitors to the Grand Canyon were the prehistoric Indians and they broke the first trails that skirted the rim or plumbed the depths. There was a pre-Columbian trade network that covered much of the Southwest and some of the trails in this network led around and through the Canyon. There were and are out-of-the-way shrines towards which pilgrims still travel. There were and are parts of the gorge where salt is mined and there were game trails along which hunters lay in wait for their quarry. Other and later inhabitants of the area broke trails by which they commuted from the arid rim to spring-watered garden plots on some of the inner-canyon plateaus. The famous Indian Gardens for instance, was, nearly within living memory, a garden plot cultivated by Havasupai who arrived via a narrow forerunner of the presentday Bright Angel Trail.[3]

The Havasupai and other Native Americans used these trails, some of which were centuries old by then, right up to the coming of the prospectors, who began to appear in noticeable numbers around 1880, drawn by the lure of mineral wealth. It was this glittering lure, plus the twofold necessity of supplying the ore's extraction and facilitating its removal for smelting and "cashing-in" that first prompted the "development" of many of the South Rim trails. The stories of these early prospectors and trail builders could be a book in itself and it is said that by the time the mining fever had abated and the plod of ore-laden burros was just a memory, there were no fewer than 84 different miners' trails into the Grand Canyon!

While space does not allow an in-depth look at all of them, the following inventory should give at least a general idea of the part played by some of them and their builders in the Canyon's latterday history.

The Tanner and Bass Trails:

The first of the prospectors to get into trail building and development in a big way were probably Seth Tanner and William W. Bass. Both men had filed claims in the Canyon by the mid-1880s and their trails date from that period. Tanner's trail, sometimes called the "Horsethief Trail" on account of its occasional use by members of that profession to move stolen stock back and forth from Utah to Arizona, was built around 1885 and begins at Lipan Point on the South Rim[4] from whence it runs down to Tanner's former silver and copper claims on the river at Tanner Canyon Rapids. At this point, the Beamer Trail, named for another earlyday prospector, begins and runs, partly along the river and partly on a terrace by way of Palisades Creek to the confluence of the Colorado and the Little Colorado rivers. This entire route, while still open to foot traffic, is classified by the Park Service as "unmaintained"—meaning that there are no facilities or regular water supplies along the route. As the "unmaintained" routes are pretty much left to take care of themselves, the would-be hiker on one would be well-advised to be in top condition, take plenty of water and emergency supplies and seek the advice of the Backcountry Office and the Park Service before setting out.

William Bass, who built or improved over 50 miles of trails in and around the Grand Canyon, refurbished parts of a network of Indian game trails to reach his mining claims and later on to convey parties of tourists. The bulk of this work survives as the "Bass Trail," presently subdivided into a "South Bass" and a "North Bass."

The South Bass begins near the former site of Bass Camp on Havasupai Point, west of Grand Canyon Village, and follows an old Havasupai trail nine miles to the river. Bass himself actually named this route the "Mystic Spring Trail," but the trail

Bass and companion in Bass tramway. *(Courtesy National Park Service, Grand Canyon National Park)*

was renamed in his honor in 1937. The South Bass now ends at the Colorado River, but in 1908 Bass constructed a tramway across the river at this point to ferry supplies and passengers to the other side. Sadly, at least from the standpoint of historical curiosity, this "cage on a cable" no longer exists. The North Bass Trail begins on the other side of the river and ascends to Swampy Point on the North Rim. The two halves of the Bass Trail are now classified as "unmaintained."

View of the Rust cable crossing (tramway) on the Colorado River, circa 1908-1910. This was near the presentday site of the suspension bridge. *(Photo courtesy National Park Service, Grand Canyon National Park)*

The Hance Trails:

John Hance, who was among the first to arrive as a prospector in the 1880s and who would remain an area fixture until his death in 1919, may have actually constructed the first of the scenic trails into the Canyon. While much of the information that he passed on to later visitors was at least highly suspect, and occasionally downright fantastic, it is reliably recorded that in 1883 Mrs. Edward E. Ayers, her daughter and a young Miss Sturgis used the Hance Trail to make their historic descent into the Canyon. The trip was historic in that Mrs. Ayers, wife of the well known Flagstaff lumberman Edward Everett Ayers, was the first white woman to complete the trip. Two years later, Ayers himself made the trip and seemed much gratified by the experience.

This original trail, usually called the "Old" Hance Trail, to distinguish it from its post-1895 successor, was something fit to try the nerves of the most dedicated traveler. In places, the descent skirted hair-raising drops and went over cliffs on ropes and rough-hewn ladders. If this route existed between 1883-1885, it was at least contemporary with Bass and Tanner's trails and it may have predated them. Given Hance's carelessness with dates and liberal interpretation of history (he was reputed to have fought on both sides in the American Civil War, although not at the same time, and once claimed to have dug the Grand Canyon itself and used the tailings to pile up the San Francisco Peaks), the truth may always be a mystery. However, since all three routes incorporated parts of Indian trails that were old when Coronado stopped by, the question of who did what first probably doesn't really matter.

The Old Hance Trail began on the rim just north of Hance's ranch and the later site of the Buggeln Hotel and followed the eastern arm of Hance Canyon into the inner gorge. This trail, which Hance was always improving (he replaced the ropes and ladders fairly early on), was destroyed by an 1895 storm which caused extensive washouts and rock slides. The route, while it has been followed in recent years by experienced hikers, is long abandoned and several stages more primitive than even the most neglected of the "unmaintained" trails.

The presentday or "New" Hance Trail officially replaced the mostly unlamented "Old" trail in the year of the great storm although it was open for business several years before that as is evidenced by the entry in the famous ***Baedeker*** guide of 1893:

> The bottom of the canyon may be reached by a new and fatiguing trail (steady head necessary) beginning ½-mile from Hance's (fee for each pers. $1; pack animal $2; guide and pack animals for 1-6 pers. $10).[5]

Cameron Camp (Indian Gardens), 1906. *(Photo courtesy National Park Service, Grand Canyon National Park)*

The New Hance Trail, which was in regular use by excursion groups as late as the 1920s, begins near Moran Point on the East Rim Drive and follows Red Canyon down to Hance Rapids on the river, eight miles below. The trail is presently classified as "unmaintained" by the Park Service.

The Cameron/Bright Angel Trail:

The next major trail to be constructed was the Cameron Trail, now called the Bright Angel. In 1891, Pete Berry, Robert Ferguson, C. H. McClure and Niles Cameron improved parts of an old Havasupai route and connected this with elements of new construction to create a trail to their mining claims in the inner gorge. Berry filed this trail as a toll road with the land authorities and the partners began levying fees on travelers, sightseers and other prospectors who used their road—a not altogether unheard of practice in the area since John Hance was doing the same thing a couple of miles east at the same time.

In 1902, Berry and Ralph Cameron (Niles' brother), who had by then bought up most of the mining interests in the area, sold most of their holdings to the Canyon Copper Company. Not included in the sale was the Cameron Trail which Ralph continued to operate as a private toll road until 1906 when he sold the route to Coconino County. The county then "hired" him as tollkeeper and he continued to pocket a healthy percentage of the take as remuneration for his services.

By this time, Ralph was under fire from the Santa Fe Railroad which had reached the Canyon in 1901. The Santa Fe and its affiliated concessionaire, The Fred Harvey Company, had their own ideas about how the Grand Canyon tourist industry should develop and these ideas did not include Ralph Cameron who they pilloried as a greedy, unscrupulous private person who was using the mining laws of the time to tie up choice pieces of public land for his own advantage.

This evaluation, while largely correct except for the relative quantities of "greedy" and "unscrupulous," remained for years only an opinion of parties who were not exactly paragons of altruism themselves. It wasn't Ralph Cameron's fault that he had gotten there first and it wasn't his fault that the mining laws of the time were a little peculiar, slanted as they were in favor of wide-open development as opposed to the conservation and preservation theories then being enacted into law and official policy by the Theodore Roosevelt administration.

What was actually causing the most discomfort to Ralph Cameron's competitors was the fact that he was operating legally and well within the laws of the time and that his position in the territorial Republican Party, which was one of great influence, made tangling with him risky, especially for those who had to court the politicians to stay in business themselves. The railroad and Fred Harvey tried though—no fewer than 19 times over the years in front of the Arizona Supreme Court, invariably without success. Finally, Cameron's toll collecting and control of Indian Gardens forced the railroad into the trail-building business itself. The fruit of this labor was the Hermit Trail from the end of the West Rim Drive down to Hermit Creek but, more about that later.

The U.S. Forest Service, which administered Grand Canyon from 1908, when the area became a National Monument, until 1919 when the National Park was created, got into the struggle as did the National Park Service later on. As agencies of the Interior Department, they should have fared better, but they didn't. Cameron's claims, which predated them both, were no more assailable in court than before and Cameron's election first to the House of Representatives, and then to the U.S. Senate (where he wound up on the appropriations committee for the Interior Department and nearly succeeded in pulling the financial plug on the Park Service one year) seemed to assure an interminable future of squabbling.

Ralph Cameron's ascendancy was not for long though. In 1927, the Park Service completed the toll-free Kaibab Trail which cut into revenues from the Cameron Trail. Then, in the senatorial race that same year, Cameron lost to Carl Hayden of Tempe. With his political clout gone by the wayside, the federal government (or that part of it that wanted him out of the way) acted by purchasing the Cameron Trail from Coconino County and firing Ralph as toll-keeper. . . and, that was the end of the Cameron toll road.

Water train on Grandview Trail, circa 1890's. *(From G. K. Woods collection, photographer unknown)*

In December, 1937, the U.S. Board of Geographic Names officially changed the trail's name from Cameron to Bright Angel. Now the most heavily traveled of the inner-canyon trails, the Bright Angel is administered and maintained by the National Park Service.

The Grand View Trail:

In June, 1892, a year after he had helped to launch the Cameron Trail, Pete Berry started his own thoroughfare. Named the "Grand View" trail, this route dropped off the rim at Grand View Point, close by the log and frame hotel of the same name (of which Berry was part owner and proprietor) and wound down to Horseshoe Mesa. Here were the copper mines from which Berry planned to make his fortune. But the dreams of wealth turned out to be fleeting, as the costs of transporting the ore to a smelter became prohibitively high and the government stepped up its campaign to discourage and force out the independent miners and prospectors from what became a Game Preserve in 1906 and a National Monument in 1908. The Grand View Hotel closed in the latter year and mining had ceased the year before that, in 1907, when Berry finally threw in the towel. Remnants of the mining operation still exist though

A resting place at the head of Grandview Trail, 1890's. *(G. K. Woods collection)*

on Horseshoe Mesa as an attraction for the occasional hiker on Berry's trail which is now classified as "unmaintained."

The Boucher Trail:

Louis D. Boucher, a French-Canadian, arrived at the Canyon around 1891 and went into the prospecting/dude wrangling business soon after. Boucher's trail dates from 1902-1905 and is therefore the last of the privately-owned trails to be built. The original trailhead was near Rowe's Well, west of the Grand Canyon Village and led by turns to Boucher's "home" camp at Dripping Spring and then down to a site about a mile from the river where, along Boucher Creek, Louis planted a 75-tree fruit orchard and a vegetable garden and ran a two-tent and one-corral tourist camp until 1912 when he left the Canyon to follow the siren call of a rich "strike" in Colorado. Until then, Boucher could often be seen riding his white mule from one part of his below-the-rim empire to another. It was said of him that he "wore a white beard, rode a white mule and told only white lies to his guests" in comparison to the also-bearded John Hance, who rode a mouse-colored mule and told epic tales that were nowhere near as white!

Scene on Hance Trail, date unknown.
(From the G. K. Woods Collection)

The Hermit Trail:

The original part of the Hermit Trail was laid down by Daniel Hogan, a transplanted New Yorker who prospected in the area in 1806. However, not much further development occurred until 1912-1913 when the Santa Fe Railroad and the Fred Harvey Company, in an effort to bypass Ralph Cameron's toll road, built the rest of what is now the Hermit Trail down to Louis Boucher's old tourist camp about an hour's walk from the river.

Boucher himself had left the Canyon in 1912 but Mary E. Jane Colter, architect of the Lookout Studio and other buildings on the rim, named the trail after him. The fact that Boucher was gone and was therefore no longer a competitor (unlike Cameron, who continued to perch like some evil genie at the head of his toll-road siphoning off business from the "legitimate" concessionaires), probably made this gracious gesture more palatable to those who were not only still around but bankrolling the construction.

Actually, Boucher, while he had been in the dude wrangling

business, had never pursued that line of endeavor with the same enthusiasm as Bass, Hance and the others. Boucher was seemingly content to keep a low profile, work his claims, tend his orchard and rescue the odd stranded river runner who might beach himself at the mouth of Boucher Creek.

Later on, a tourist camp named "Hermit Camp" (also by Colter for Boucher) was run here by the railroad and Fred Harvey as an overnight stop on the longer cross-canyon trips. Here, before 1931, was a small tent village complete with piped-in water and an aerial tramway that brought supplies down from Pima Point on the rim. Here, too, was the home of one of the Southwest's more unique taxi services. A Model-T Ford was disassembled and sent down in the tramway for reassembly at the canyon bottom. Once down there, it was used to ferry cargo from the tramway terminus to the tourist camp (the tram did *not* carry passengers). This "tin Lizzie" was the first, so far the last, and probably the only motor vehicle ever to be operated at the bottom of the Grand Canyon.[6]

Cottonwood trees were planted and in its heyday, the camp was quite a bustling and picturesque place. When Phantom Ranch was developed on Bright Angel Creek as an alternative cross-canyon stop though, Hermit Camp was abandoned and nothing remains there today.

The Hermit Trail begins behind Hermit's Rest at the end of the West Rim Drive and descends the east wall of the Hermit Basin Natural Area[7] to the site of the old camp. There is a secondary trail from there to the river.

The North and South Kaibab Trails:

While Louis Boucher was the last individual to build an inner-canyon trail whose work has survived in whole or in part to the present day, the Kaibab Trail system is the work of the National Park Service and dates from the 1920s.

In 1924, the upper management echelons of the Park Service, after noticing with some enthusiasm that the Hermit Trail had made inroads on Ralph Cameron's toll revenues; and, noticing too (with somewhat less enthusiasm) that Cameron was now a powerful United States' Senator who might be in office for years

Hikers and horseback group at Ribbon Falls, 1926.
(From the author's collection)

or live forever—maybe both—decided to build another alternative to the operation of their old nemesis. The result was the South Kaibab or Yaki Trail[8] which begins at Yaki Point, 4½ miles east of Grand Canyon Village, and drops steeply down to follow Cedar Ridge into the inner gorge where it crosses a suspension bridge across the Colorado River and ends at the mouth of Bright Angel Creek close by Phantom Ranch. The North Kaibab Trail begins here (or ends, depending on whether you're coming or going) and follows Bright Angel Creek to Roaring Springs Canyon and then winds up to the North Rim.

The Tonto Trail:

This route, while not exactly one of the "historic" trails, does connect most of the rim-to-river trails from the South Rim as it skirts the edge of the Tonto Plateau along the inner gorge on its way from the mouth of Red Canyon at Hance Rapids downstream to Garnet Canyon. This trail, subdivided into an "East Tonto," "Tonto" and "West Tonto," is more than 90 miles long, much of the distance being taken up by the windings in and out of side canyons along the way. The name for the trail was first proposed in March 1906, by the U.S. Geological Survey to honor the Tonto Apaches.

The North Rim Trails:

While the North Rim of the Grand Canyon boasts scenery second to none, the climate of the area (1,000 to 1,500 feet higher on the average than the South Rim) and its comparative isolation have held the development of tourist facilities to the bare minimum. Even today, the North Rim receives only a fraction of the crowds that flock to the South Rim facilities. While the area was explored by the Indians and there was some prospecting in the early days, the absence of facilities for ore transportation to smelters and the lack of settled supply centers in the Arizona Strip ruled out commercial development of any degree and the trails which descend into the depths of the Canyon from the North Rim today are of fairly recent origin—in most cases, dating from after the creation of the national park.

Among these may be mentioned the Thunder River, the Bill

Hikers on Bright Angel Point in 1926. Photo was taken near the present site of Grand Canyon Lodge.
(Photo from the author's collection)

Hall, the Nankoweap[9], and the Clear Creek trails, in addition to the already-mentioned North Kaibab and North Bass. As access to any of these from the North Rim is practically limited to the warm-weather months when the roads leading into the North Rim park areas are open, anyone wanting to follow these routes would be well-advised to check with the Backcountry Reservation Office and the Park Service before setting out.

Besides these historic and scenic routes associated with the Indians and the prospectors and the development of the tourist industry at the Grand Canyon, there are a number of lesser-known but no less interesting trails within the national park boundaries and several are described in Harvey Butchart's books listed in the *Bibliography/Reading List* at the end of this work.

Thomas E. Way, Jr.

Notes

1. Day rides on privately-owned stock are permissible anytime, although a permit from the Backcountry Reservation Office is required for overnight rides. Also, the private owner is responsible for packing in feed for his or her animals. Corrals exist at both the South Kaibab and Bright Angel trailheads as well as in the Canyon at Phantom Ranch and a campground laid out with the particular needs of the private horse owner is at least in the planning stages as this book goes to press. Also planned is a printed handout which will be a joint composition of the Arizona Horsemen's Association and the National Park Service. This should be available early in 1990 and will contain information for the horse owner and various regulations. In the meantime, information on use of privately-owned stock at Grand Canyon can be had from the Backcountry Reservation Office.

2. Grand Canyon Trail Guides, a concessionaire of the National Park Service.

3. In 1939-40, the compilers of ***Arizona, The Grand Canyon State***, a guide book published by the Writer's Program of the WPA, interviewed Big Jim Vesner, chief of the Havasupai. Big Jim, who appeared in print as "Lŏng Jim" (an evident case of mistaken identity or confusion with the pioneer sheepherder, Long Jim, who had an area canyon named for him), said that he had been born at what is now Indian Gardens and remembered his parents going to Prescott "to verify rumors that there were men with white faces." As Prescott was first settled in the early 1860s, Big Jim was probably at least in his 80s when the WPA researchers found him and got their interview. At this time, the old chief's formal wear included a frock coat and top hat and a World War I medal presented to him by the Queen of the Belgians and he must have made a splendid picture as he recounted his life story to the writers.

   At that time, the Havasupai were camped at Rowe's Well in a tent and brush arbor community whose population varied in numbers according to the seasons and who was coming or going to and from the tribe's real home in Havasu Canyon. Most of today's Havasupai live in and around Supai Village, in their canyon reservation beyond the borders of the national park, although in the past the tribe ranged as far as the Little Colorado Valley, east of the San Francisco Peaks, where the Hopi called them "Cosninos." In 1776, Garces found most of them at home in Havasu Canyon, but there were a few stragglers in the Little Colorado Valley as late as 1850. When John Wesley Powell visited there in 1870, a Havasupai chief showed him ruins once inhabited by fellow tribesmen. Intertribal conflict and the incursions of the white men drove the Havasupai to their present canyon home where their reservation dates from 1880. In 1975, after prolonged litigation, the tribe regained control over some territory on the rim and surrounding plateau.

   SOURCES: ***Arizona, The Grand Canyon State.*** Writer's Program, WPA. Hastings House, NY. 1940. Page 492. ***Arizona Place Names***. Barnes (1960 Granger ed.). UA Press, Tucson. Page 146.

4. Lipan Point is on the East Rim Drive between the Tusayan Museum and Desert View. Formerly known as Lincoln Point, it was renamed in 1902 to honor the Lipan Indians, a tribe that once ranged in western Texas.

5. Quoted from ***The United States, With an Excursion Into Mexico, a Handbook For Travellers, 1893.*** Karl Baedeker (editor). Facsimile edition by the Da Capo Press, NY. 1971. Page 413.

6. The Model-T that operated at Hermit Camp was the only automobile to operate so far into the Canyon, although those who drove their flivvers (and those who

continue to drive their vehicles) on the road from Peach Springs to the head of Diamond Creek near the old Farlee Hotel can also claim to have driven at the bottom of the Grand Canyon.

7. The Boucher and Dripping Spring Trails descend the western wall of this basin. Descriptions of this area can be found in the Butchart and Weir books listed in the *Bibliography/Reading List*.

8. "Yaki" is a corruption of "Yaqui" and refers to Yaki Point, the trailhead of the South Kaibab or Yaki Trail. The point was named about 1910 to honor the Yaqui Indians of Old Mexico who were about to be forcibly relocated to a reservation far from their traditional homes. Many of the Yaqui fled to the United States at this time and settled in southern Arizona.

9. The Nankoweap Trail, since it was laid out under the direction of John Wesley Powell in the 1880s, and used as a link with the Tanner and Beamer Trails from the South Rim, is an historical route and therefore an exception to the "recent origin" rule.

Grand View Hotel. *(Photo National Park Service, Grand Canyon National Park)*

"Tally-ho" loaded with sightseers on rim of Grand Canyon about 1903. *(Photo courtesy Santa Fe Railway)*

Grand Canyon Stage in front of Bank Hotel, Flagstaff. *(Photo courtesy Arizona Historical Society, Pioneer Museum, Flagstaff)*

Bibliography/Reading List

BOOKS:

Annerino, John. ***Hiking the Grand Canyon.*** Sierra Club Books, San Francisco. 1986.

Baedeker, Karl (editor). ***The United States, With an Excursion Into Mexico, a Handbook For Travellers, 1893.*** Facsimile edition by the Da Capo Press, NY. 1971.

Barnes, Will C. ***Arizona Place Names.*** The Byrd Granger edition from UA Press, Tucson. 1960.

Butchart, Harvey. ***Grand Canyon Treks.*** La Siesta Press, Glendale, California. 1970.

Cline, Platt. ***They Came To the Mountain.*** NAU and Northland Press, Flagstaff. 1976.

Granger, Byrd Howell. ***Arizona's Names, X Marks the Place.*** The Falconer Publishing Co. 1983.

Hughes, J. Donald. ***In the House of Stone and Light.*** Grand Canyon Natural History Association. 1978.

James, George Wharton. ***The Grand Canyon of Arizona: How To See It.*** Little, Brown and Co., Boston. 1910.

Keithley, Ralph. ***Buckey O'Neill.*** The Caxton Printers, Ltd., Caldwell, Idaho. 1949.

Kolb, Ellsworth L. ***Through the Grand Canyon From Wyoming to Mexico.*** The Macmillan Co., NY. 1920.

Lavender, David. ***River Runners of the Grand Canyon.*** Grand Canyon Natural History Association and UA Press, Tucson. 1985.

Manns, Timothy. ***A Guide to Grand Canyon Village Historical District.*** Grand Canyon Natural History Association. 1980 edition.

Nims, Franklin A. ***The Photographer and the River, 1889-1890; The Colorado Canyon Diary of Franklin A. Nims With the Brown-Stanton Railroad Survey Expedition.*** Stagecoach Press, Santa Fe. 1967.

Theobald, John Orr and Lillian. ***Arizona Territory: Post Offices and Postmasters.*** Arizona Historical Foundation, Phoenix. 1961.

Woods, G. K. (compiler). ***Personal Impressions of the Grand Canon of the Colorado River, Near Flagstaff, Arizona as Seen Through Nearly Two-thousand Eyes, and Written In the Private Visitors' Book of the World-famous Guide Captain John Hance, Guide, Story-teller and Path-Finder. Collected and Compiled by G. K. Woods.*** Published for G. K. Woods, Flagstaff, A. T. by the Whitaker and Ray Co., San Francisco. 1899.

Workers of the Writers' Program of the Work Projects Administration in the State of Arizona (compilers). ***Arizona, The Grand Canyon State, A State Guide.*** Hastings House, NY. 1940.

PERIODICALS:

Chappell, Gordon. "Railroad at the Rim, The Origin and Growth of Grand Canyon Village." ***The Journal of Arizona History***, Vol. 17, No. 1 (Spring, 1976). pp. 89-107.

Fuchs, James R. "A History of Williams, Arizona, 1876-1951." Originally published as ***Social Science Bulletin 23, U of A Bulletin,*** Vol. XXIV, No. 5 (Nov. 1953). 168 pages.

King, June O'Neill. "Grand Days of the Grandview." ***Mountain Living***. June 1986. 2 pages.

Matthews, John. "The Grand Canyon Caper." ***Arizona Highways.*** August 1977. pp. 36-41.

Spector, Michael. "Road to the River." ***Arizona Highways.*** November 1978. pp. 38-41.

Strong, Douglas Hillman. "The Man Who 'Owned' Grand Canyon." ***The American West***, Vol. 6, No. 5 (September 1969). pp. 33-40.

Udall, Stewart S. (text) and Jerry Jacka (photography). "In Coronado's Footsteps." ***Arizona Highways***. April 1984. pp. 3-43.

Wahler, Charles B. "The Flagstaff to Grand Canyon Stage." ***The Grand Canyon Guide***, Vol. 2, No. 8 (July 2-15, 1978). pp. 1 and 2.

Wahmann, Russell. "Grand Canyon Stage Line." ***Desert Magazine of the Southwest.*** January 1975. pp. 32-35.

UNPUBLISHED MANUSCRIPTS:

Verkamp, Margaret M. ***History of Grand Canyon National Park.*** Unpublished MA Thesis. University of Arizona, Tucson. 1940.

NEWSPAPERS:

Arizona Republic. Phoenix, Arizona.

Arizona Weekly Miner. Prescott, A. T. (no longer published)

Coconino Sun. Flagstaff, Arizona (predecessor of the ***Arizona Daily Sun***)

Williams News. Williams, Arizona.

PERSONAL INTERVIEWS

Much of the information that I obtained from interviews and conversations was accumulated piecemeal over the years between my own arrival in the Williams-Grand Canyon area in 1917 and the present. For this reason, there are no exact "date of interview" notations with the name entries. Also, many of the people listed below are no longer living.

C. E. Albert: AT&SF station agent, Williams Arizona.

W. Leo Black: Railroad engineer on the Grand Canyon line.

Harry Boulin: Farrier and blacksmith at the Fred Harvey mule barn, Grand Canyon.

Eldon Bowman: Flagstaff resident who contributed information on the use of privately-owned horses at Grand Canyon today.

Martin Buggeln: A&P railroader, transportation pioneer and businessman/entrepreneur of earlyday Williams and Grand Canyon.

Clarke and Laura Cole: Longtime Williams residents.

Harry and Ethel Cole: Longtime residents of Williams and Grand Canyon.

Les Cravey: Pioneer trail guide and resident of Grand Canyon.

Mary Lockridge Cravey: Lifelong resident, pioneer and historian at Grand Canyon and Williams.

Glenn W. Irwin: AT&SF station agent, Williams, Arizona.

James Kennedy: Pioneer and early town marshal of Williams.

Seth Lilly: Grand Canyon transportation pioneer.

Harry Matson: AT&SF ticket agent and lifelong resident of the Williams-Grand Canyon area, including the lumber camps at Apex and Bellemont.

N. S. "Sandy" McLean: Railroad engineer on the Grand Canyon line.

Ambrose Means: Williams area pioneer and guide for one of Theodore Roosevelt's hunting trips to the North Rim.

Dr. Dermont W. Melick, M.D.: Physician and surgeon of Williams and Phoenix.

Dr. P. A. Melick, M.D.: Pioneer physician of Williams.

Grace Lockridge Moore: Lifelong resident, pioneer and historian of the Williams-Grand Canyon area.

Robert O'Hara: Sales Manager, Grand Canyon National Park Lodges, Grand Canyon.

Helen Pearson: Longtime Williams resident, writer and historian.

Lilo M. Perrin: Pioneer sheep and cattleman of northern Arizona.

Kenneth M. Polson: Lifelong resident of Williams, son of a pioneer merchant family and bus driver on the Williams-Grand Canyon run.

George Reinhart: Railroad engineer on the Grand Canyon line.

Pauline Samson: Stepdaughter of Ed Hamilton and longtime Williams resident.

M. E. Spivey: AT&SF track supervisor.

Rouby H. Sullivant: Longtime Williams resident and historian.

Sidney "Sid" Terry: Railroad engineer on the Grand Canyon Line.

Jack Tooker: Railroad engineer on the Grand Canyon Line.

John "Jack" Verkamp: Pioneer, lifelong resident of and merchant at Grand Canyon.

Margaret "Peggy" Verkamp: Pioneer educator and historian of Grand Canyon.

CORRESPONDENCE:

Robert E. Gehrt: Vice President, Public Relations, Santa Fe Pacific Corporation, Chicago, Illinois

Louis Tisdale of Phoenix, Arizona, past president and member of the Board of Directors of the Arizona Museum, Phoenix, Arizona.

Modern 18-foot oared boat in Hance Rapids. *(Photo courtesy Expeditions, Inc., Flagstaff)*

View of auto camp at Rowe's Well, circa 1920. *(Photo courtesy of Mrs. Helen Polson, Williams)*

Index

ORDER BLANK

Golden West Publishers

4113 N. Longview Ave. Phoenix, AZ 85014

Please ship the following books:

Number of Copies		Per Copy	AMOUNT
	Arizona Adventure	5.00	
	Arizona Hideaways	4.50	
	Arizona—Off the Beaten Path	5.00	
	Arizona Outdoor Guide	5.00	
	Bill Williams Mountain Men	5.00	
	Conflict at the Border	5.00	
	Cowboy Country Cartoons	4.50	
	Cowboy Slang	5.00	
	Destination: Grand Canyon	5.00	
	Explore Arizona	5.00	
	Fools' Gold	5.00	
	Ghost Towns in Arizona	4.50	
	In Old Arizona	5.00	
	Mavericks	5.00	
	Old West Adventures in Arizona	5.00	
	On the Arizona Road	5.00	
	Other Mexico, The	9.00	
	Prehistoric Arizona	5.00	
	Southwest Saga...	5.00	
Add $1.00 to total order for shipping & handling			$1.00

Check (or money order) enclosed...$__________

Name ______________________________

Address ______________________________

City ______________ State ______ Zip ________

This order blank may be photo-copied.

Books from Golden West Publishers

The Other Mexico—Revel in ancient treasures and modern pleasures with world traveler E. J. Guarino, your host to the myriad museums and archaeological ruins in today's Mexico. 90 full-color photographs, plus maps, site-plans, index. (176 pages). . .***$9.00***

Cowboy Country Cartoons—a cartoon excursion through the whimsical west of renowned cowboy cartoonist-sculptor Jim Willoughby. Western humor at its ribald best! (128 pages). . .***$4.50***

Southwestern frontier tales more thrilling than fiction. Trimble brings history to life with humor, pathos and irony of pioneer lives: territorial politics, bungled burglaries, shady deals, frontier lawmen, fighting editors, Baron of Arizona, horse and buggy doctors, etc. ***In Old Arizona*** by Marshall Trimble (160 pages). . .***$5.00***

Southwest Saga—the way it really was, by Southwest historian-journalism William C. McGaw—Esteban's life among the Zuni, Pancho Villa's raid north of the border, Mark Twain's drug scheme, the strange death of Ambrose Bierce, etc. (160 pages). . .***$5.00***

Ride the back trails with modern-day mountain men, as they preserve the memory of Arizona's rugged adventurers of the past. Buckskin-clad, the mountain men stage annual treks from Williams, AZ all the way to Phoenix, AZ and to other destinations. Hilarious anecdotes of hard-riding men. ***Bill Williams Mountain Men*** by Thomas E. Way (128 pages). . .***$5.00***

Books from Golden West Publishers

Men played for keeps in the Arizona Territory... where romance of stagecoach routes was interrupted by murder from ambush...where raiding was a way of life...where ranchers and rustlers had scores to settle...place names that still ring with vibrant memories of a glorious past... recaptured for all time in the pages of ***Old West Adventures in Arizona*** by Charles D. Lauer (160 pages)...$5.00

Discover arrowheads, old coins, bottles, fossil beds, old forts, petroglyphs, ruins, lava tubes, waterfalls, ice caves, cliff dwellings and other Arizona wonders. Detailed maps and text invite you to vist 60 hidden, out-of-the way places. ***Explore Arizona!*** by Rick Harris (128 pages)... $5.00

Visit the silver cities of Arizona's golden past with this prize-winning reporter-photographer. Come along to the towns whose heydays were once wild and wicked! Crumbling adobe walls, old mines, cemeteries, cabins and castles. ***Ghosts Towns and Historical Haunts in Arizona*** by Thelma Heatwole (144 pages)...$4.50

The saga of centuries-old search for Spanish gold and the Lost Dutchman Mine continues. Facts, myths and legends of fabled Superstition Mountains told by a geologist who was there. Mysteries of lost hopes, lost lives—lost gold! ***Fool's Gold*** by Robert Sikorsky (144 pages)... $5.00

The American cowboy had a way with words! Lingo of the American West, captured in 2000 phrases and expressions—colorful, humorous, earthy, raunchy! Includes horse and cattle terms, rodeo talk, barb wire names, cattle brands. ***Cowboy Slang*** by "Frosty" Potter, illustrated by Ron Scofield (128 pages)...$5.00

Meet the Author!

Thomas E. "Spike" Way grew up at the time the auto and the trains were vying for supremacy in transportation to the Grand Canyon.

Consequently, he was acquainted with many of the train crews by being a part-time "call boy." It was the call boy's job to call the engine crews to man the engines and to help move the heavy trains over the mountain grades.

Way missed being a native Arizonan by eight years. Born in Boyne City, Michigan, he was transplanted to Williams, Arizona, at a tender age and has lived there ever since.

He attended Northern Arizona Teacher's College (now Northern Arizona University) in Flagstaff, Arizona, and was employed for a time by the Saginaw-Manistee Lumber Company. He drove a Union Oil truck and was a free-lance writer for the *Williams News*.

As Justice of the Peace, Magistrate and Coroner in Williams for 35 years, Way listened to stories by and about the old timers. These provided him with material for his writings.

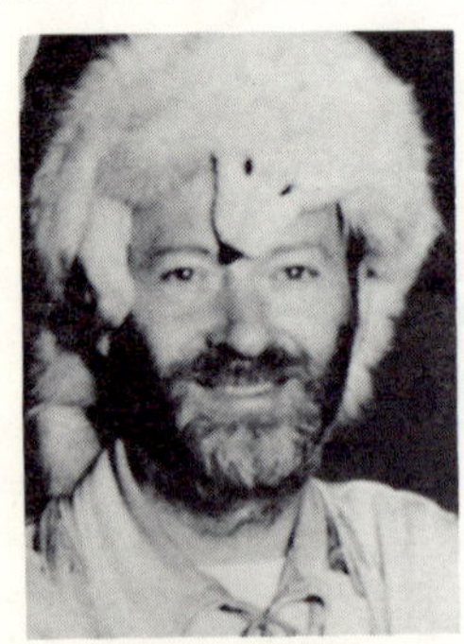

The author in "Bill Williams" garb

In his book, *Bill Williams Mountain Men*, published by Golden West in 1987, the author narrated the activities and antics of Bill Williams' modern-day counterparts as they rode the back trails clad in buckskins, astride rough-coated mounts.

In *Destination: Grand Canyon*, he traces the development of all forms of travel to the Grand Canyon of the Colorado River to the present.